# CHOOSE YOUʀ THOUGHTS

## CREATING A BETTER LIFE FROM THE POWER OF YOUR MIND

T.K. ALANA

# CONTENTS

*Introduction*                                        5

1. Understanding Your Thoughts                        11
2. Beyond Positive Thinking                           22
3. The Power of Mindfulness                           34
4. Mindful Meditation                                 48
5. The Power of Gratitude                             81
6. The Power of the Body                              108

*How to Make Lasting Changes in the Way You           121
Think*

*Conclusion*                                          137
*References*                                          141

# INTRODUCTION

---

*"Nurture your mind with great thoughts, for you will never go any higher than you think."*

*— BENJAMIN DISRAELI (DESCHENE, N.D.)*

---

It's a familiar story. You wake up in the morning and struggle to get out of bed. You go through the day, and the stress you feel is overwhelming. You feel that every day is a challenge, and you know that if you could "just think positive," you would feel mentally, physically, and emotionally better. The problem, however, is you've tried affirmations every morning and have changed some of your negative thoughts into positive ones; but it just doesn't seem to be really working.

The truth is, it doesn't work for a long period of time because there are certain methods that you should follow to help your mind make the switch. The process goes deeper than merely noticing when you're thinking negatively and trying to think positive. My book explains this process. It is about how you can change your life by changing your thoughts. It explains how thoughts affect our feelings, decisions, and actions, and subsequently, our lives.

You might be asking yourself, "Why should I read this book?" or "What can I gain from this book to help change my thought patterns?" The key is that this book not only helps you understand your thought pattern and where it comes from but enables you to overcome real-life obstacles. I'll show you why certain strategies work, through studies and real-life examples. I have been there too. I was once a negative thinker who struggled to have positive thoughts. I spent many sleepless nights wondering what was wrong with me, only to find out that it wasn't me - it was my thought pattern, and I just needed to find a way to choose my thoughts that worked for me.

You should also read this book because having negative thoughts can lead to issues, such as anxiety, low self-esteem, and depression. The thoughts start because you're thinking about the mistakes you made in the past that make you feel ashamed. You feel anxiety about the present, or begin to fear the unknown of the future. Once you become trapped in one of these three reasons, your mind begins to wander down a dark road. You have unhelpful thoughts about yourself, your life, and other people. For example, you'll label yourself as "dumb" when you make a mistake, or you'll tell yourself that you "need to become a better person" for anyone to like you.

These harmful thought patterns will affect not only your self-esteem, but also your career and how you make decisions. They can even affect your ability to complete tasks because negativity makes it harder to focus, and you lack motivation. Other ways that will affect your career include:

- Increasing your tendency toward procrastination.
- Believing your projects need to be perfect, but always feeling like they're never "good enough."
- You are struggling to socialize with your co-worker and finding yourself withdrawing from social activities.
- You try to please everyone.
- You constantly feel exhausted.
- You hide from your problems instead of meeting them head-on.
- You can't handle criticism.
- You struggle to reach your goals and might even stop setting them in the first place.
- You don't take risks.

- You become indecisive and let everyone else make decisions for you.

- You decline a promotion or new leadership roles because you feel you won't measure up.

Another impact of your negative thought patterns and low self-esteem is your relationships, whether with your family, friends, or romantic partner. Self-esteem, which is how you view yourself, will impact your relationships because you can see them a certain way as well. For example, what if you have trouble making decisions about your career, hobbies, and relationships? Your partner wants to come up with a plan for financial goals over the next year. They want to have enough money saved up for a down payment for a house. Even though you have a lot of credit card debt you'd like to pay off, you struggle to decide if you want to pay off debt or help save for a home. Because your partner seems set on their decision, you agree to it. They ask you if it's really what you want because you don't look sure, but you continue to tell them that you accept and try to show your enthusiasm and excitement.

This might seem like a small detail in your relationship, but it can cause problems down the road. You'll continue to make decisions this way and, without proper communication with your partner, they'll start to come up to their own conclusions. Eventually, they will begin to pull away from the relationship. The biggest problem in this scenario is that you don't realize what is happening until it might be too late.

Another way negative thoughts can interfere with relationships is through accepting other people, whether it's their
culture, way of living, sexual orientation, or ethnicity. When
you struggle to accept yourself, it's easy for you to judge other
people and struggle to accept them. This can cause you to
strive for control in a personal relationship to protect yourself, such as making unreasonable rules or demands. Even
though you psychologically understand that people change
over time, you don't trust yourself or others to change for the
better. Your self-esteem can also cause damage through a lack
of confidence, labeling your partner, and unknowingly
lowering the self-esteem of another person through constant
criticism.

You also need to learn how to choose your thoughts because
negative thinking can take a toll on your physical health. It's
important to remember that your physical, emotional, and
mental health is all tied together. While you can get sick and
continue to feel emotionally happy, sadness can cause you to
become ill. Your immune system doesn't have the energy and
nutrition it needs to fight off an infection when your mind and
body feel "blue" or "down in the dumps" all or most of the time.

There is a lot of other helpful information that you will gain
from reading this book, such as:

• Understanding your thoughts and why you think the
  way you do.

- Dissecting through your fears and addressing them head-on.
- An introduction to meditation and how to clear your head.
- Other useful mind exercises to reframe your thinking.
- Being in complete control of your thoughts.

Wherever you are in your journey toward self-fulfillment and self-actualization, the steps in this book can help you tap into positive thinking to bring you peace of mind. We'll talk about different ways you can start to shift your thinking from negative to positive - from destructive to instructive. All of this takes time, and it won't always be easy. But, when you can choose your thoughts to be positive, you'll find that life becomes more manageable, and things that would usually get you down feel more like speed bumps instead of tragedies.

Let's get started! Take a deep breath - and begin...

1

# UNDERSTANDING YOUR THOUGHTS

*"You must be the change you wish to see in the world."*

— MAHATMA GANDHI ("21 DEEP
QUOTES ON POSITIVE THINKING,"
2016)

Have you ever been working on a project when you suddenly hear an intruder say, "You're not doing this right, everyone is going to hate it, you're not the right person for the job."? You look up knowing that the intruder is you. These are your thoughts that jump out at you and make you feel like you're a failure. Even when someone compliments you, the intruder still comes, and you wonder why. Meet your saboteur. Why do your thoughts bring you down?

The first thing you need to understand about thoughts is that they are energy. This means that they can reverberate through to your body as well as in your environment. For example, when you find yourself criticizing your project, it doesn't mean that anyone said these words to you about this particular project. It could mean that someone criticized you in the past, and this situation created an energetic field around your thoughts. Maybe your parents were highly critical of you during your childhood, or your partner criticizes everything you do. Perhaps you left a job where your supervisor never liked your work, so you feel that your new boss will react the same way.

## REASONS FOR NEGATIVE THINKING

There are several reasons for negative thinking, and many of them are significant to you. You might understand where some of your dark thoughts come from, or you might question why they come to you. Before you can start to transform your thoughts, you need to understand the causes.

Some negative thoughts will come because of certain states of mind. For example, anxiety or depression often involves recurring negative thoughts that are sometimes hard to switch to positive because you start to believe what your thoughts are telling you. These thoughts might explain to you all the unfortunate events that can unfold during the day because you don't know how to react.

It's important to note that this book is not meant to help you through any negative thoughts that form from mental health illnesses. The best step to take to help you overcome these negative thoughts is to contact a psychologist who understands your illness and can help you find the best therapy for you. By seeking therapy and using techniques discussed in this book, you'll overcome your challenge and start to see the world in a new light.

Another reason for negative thoughts is shame about the past. It's normal to toss and turn during the night thinking about the mistakes you made that day, last week, or even several years ago. For example, you think about what you told your partner during a fight and wish you could take it back. You start to think about how you could change, so you don't speak in anger again. You then begin remembering other times that you spoke out of frustration and doubted your ability to be the best spouse and parent you strive to be.

The way we think about our past shows us how powerful your negative thoughts can become. Take a moment to think about how often you dwell on your previous mistakes and failures compared to how often you think about your successes. For instance, how often do you lay in bed at night and think about how you graduated from high school or college? Do you think about all the positive statements you made or events that happened that day, last week, or last year? No, it's more common for you to fill your mind with your regrets, what hurts you; maybe you even see yourself as a failure because this is how your mind operates.

Your anxiety about the present is another reason for your negative thoughts. While it's normal to have some anxiety, you might worry too much about situations that really don't matter, such as what people think about you and if you're doing a good job at work. When you think about each situation, your mind brings out the worst-case scenario. For example, you'll tell yourself that your supervisor doesn't like your work, and your co-workers don't like you. You might lead yourself to believe that when people are whispering around you, they're talking negatively about the way you look or talk.

Once your anxiety gets out of control, you feel that it's impossible to keep your hands on the steering wheel. For example, you'll question your abilities and wonder if you're taking the right steps. Your thoughts are consistently negative, even when something positive happens. You received the employee of the month award at your job, but this doesn't mean that you didn't think that "everything will go downhill from here" or "they only gave me this award because they felt sorry for me." Anxiety can make you believe that you don't deserve the good events in your life. When the positivity does come, your anxiety will tell you this is a warning because once good events happen, negative events follow.

Negative thoughts also come from overthinking. It's important to take your time and think about all your options when making an important decision. But when you start to obsess about every detail, your mind goes into the direction of gloom. For example, you will begin to feel that no matter what decision you make, it won't be the right one. This can lead you to putting less effort into your project, missing deadlines, or even worse situations.

## WHEN YOUR THOUGHTS TALK NEGATIVELY

You know some of the most common causes of negative thinking, so now it's time to talk about when (and what) your thoughts are communicating to you. One of the key factors to changing your thinking is to note when negative thinking happens so you can take action.

You'll want to spend time reflecting on your day, the decisions you've made, and the steps you took toward your goals. Introspection is a positive self-reflection. It's healthy, but it can also lead you down a vicious cycle of negative thinking if you don't watch for negative rumination signs. For example, you're thinking about how you finished a project at work and the emotions you felt. You also remember how proud your supervisor was to see your hard work, and he or she praised your dedication. But this doesn't stop you from thinking about the awkward moments you had throughout the process, and these can start to overshadow the positivity.

One of the best steps to take when you find yourself partaking in negative rumination is to take action. You need to come up with a plan to decrease your negative thoughts and focus more on positive thinking. Your plan can include identifying your triggers, signs of negative thinking (like neck tightness, grinding teeth, insomnia), and how to start changing your thoughts. You also need to make sure that you're gentle with yourself. Don't become frustrated or angry with your negative thoughts. Instead, focus on the positive side. For instance, if you're thinking about a mistake you made, change your thinking to how you can learn from the mistake and then move on, so you don't continue to dwell on it.

You have a critical inner voice. It's something that everyone has, and you hear it from time to time. It rarely has anything positive to say about what you do, say, or even think. It's self-critical, self-denying, paranoid, and suspicious. The biggest problem is when this voice becomes all-consuming. Then, it controls your thoughts, making you believe that you can never do anything right. It can, and will decrease your self-esteem, self-worth while increasing your negative thoughts.

From the critical voice comes these types of negative self-talk. Do any of them feel familiar?

- Labeling is when you attach a label to yourself or someone else. For example, you don't perform well on your exam, so you tell yourself, "I am stupid" or "I'm not smart enough for school." You'll also look at other people and think, "They're perfect" or "They're smarter than me."

- "Should" and "must" are words that often lead to high or unrealistic expectations. Telling yourself, "I should do this" or "I must not do this" makes you believe that you need to follow these statements to succeed. However, it's rare for people to jump up and stop or start a habit immediately. It always takes time, and you need to develop a plan to give yourself time so you can be successful.

- Catastrophizing is when you blow a situation out of proportion. For example, you leave a job interview and start going over all the mistakes you think you made. You then begin to imagine that the hiring committee you interviewed with is making fun of your answers and won't even take the time to call you and say you didn't get the job.

- All or nothing is also referred to as black and white thinking. There is no middle ground or a gray area. For example, you tell yourself, "If I don't get hired for this position, my whole career is over."

- A mental filter is when you ignore the full picture and only focus on the negatives. You tend to focus on failures and not the successes that you have in your life. For example, you completed the report, but you didn't have time to proofread it with great detail, and you missed a few typos.

- Mind reading is when you believe you know what someone else is thinking. For example, "I know that he doesn't like me," or you think, "My supervisor believes that I'm not suitable for my position."

- Personalization is when you unfairly blame yourself or other people for certain situations. For example, you receive a poor grade on your exam, so you blame your parents for not helping you study the night before.

## UNDERSTANDING YOUR THINKING PATTERNS

It's important to be aware of the thinking patterns you have and how often you think a certain way. For example, how many times a day do you focus on positive over negative thinking? You probably don't usually analyze your thoughts, but you need to know your common thinking patterns so you can understand how they're affecting you. One way to do this is by keeping a thoughts journal; here, you take time to write down your thoughts, emotions associated with them, and why you thought this way. You can do this at the end of your day, but it's best to take time as soon as you notice the thought so you can analyze the situation thoroughly.

Once you understand where your patterns are mentally sitting, you can start focusing on changing your thoughts. The first step is to understand why you think the way you do.

Your thinking might come from your negative belief system. You develop this system through negative experiences in your childhood, career, and interactions with other people. The longer you think a certain way, the harder it becomes to change your belief system, and ultimately, your thoughts.

For instance, let's say you grew up in a home where your mother felt abandoned by your father, not because he wasn't around but because he rarely paid attention to her. He never complimented the way she looked, the food she cooked, or how she kept a clean house. She felt he watched television more than he talked to her, even during important conversations. Your thought pattern developed in this environment. You believe that most men don't pay attention to their partner, and you're destined to feel abandoned as your mother felt. Even when you find someone who will turn off the television during a conversation and raves about your cooking, you think that it won't last. You might even start to believe that your partner is hiding something from you and become paranoid about the reason for their positive behavior.

You might think a certain way because it's a coping mechanism, which is a strategy you use when faced with stress, painful emotions, or trauma. For example, you might avoid arguments in your relationship because your parents always argued, making you uncomfortable and scared. You develop many coping strategies early in life and carry them with you. They help you when you need to interact with other people. You also rely on your strategies to get through difficult situations. Because you've held on to your strategies for so long, you don't even really realize that you have them.

Your emotions and thought patterns work together and feed off each other. Negative thoughts will bring out paralyzing emotions that cause fear, nervousness, confusion, stress, anxiety, and anger. The longer you think negatively, the more your thoughts will affect your relationships, mental health, physical health, emotional health, and career.

Your relationships are affected because you find yourself thinking the worst about the other person or yourself. For instance, you feel that you're too much of a loner to have a healthy romantic relationship. You might believe that your partner will leave you over someone smarter or prettier. Your relationship with your children is affected because you can't meet their emotional needs. People might start to feel that you're too distant or become distant because of your negative thoughts.

Your overall health is affected, including your mental, physical, and emotional health. You start to lack self-esteem, which makes you feel worthless. From there, you can feel depressed, which leads to poor health because your immune system can't fight off colds, flu, and other illnesses. The outcome of this downfall is higher stress, anxiety, and depression.

Your career is affected because you lack motivation. You don't believe that you're "good enough" or "smart enough." You might start to think that other people are against you or that your supervisor should have hired a better employee. You will begin to feel that you're a failure, and everything you worked for is disappearing before your eyes.

Because bad thoughts can severely impact various aspects of your life, you need to improve your thoughts. By doing this, you'll start to improve your life. Your overall health will increase as you start to gain confidence. Your immune system will continue to fight off diseases, and your relationships will see better days. You'll understand that couples argue, and it's healthy as long as you keep calm and talk through the disagreement. Most importantly, your thought pattern will become positive, and you will find yourself thinking less negatively as time goes on. Soon, you will catch your negative thoughts as they happen and easily revert them into positive ones.

# 2

# BEYOND POSITIVE THINKING

---

*"There is only one corner of the universe; you can be certain of improving, and that's your own self."*

— ALDOUS HUXLEY (21 DEEP QUOTES ON POSITIVE THINKING, 2016).

---

Y ou can search Google for inspirational memes or scroll through Facebook or Instagram to get a variety of affirmation messages that tell you to "think positive" every morning. While these are helpful strategies you can incorporate into your life to help you focus more on positive thinking, the memes can make you believe that all you need to do is simply switch the direction of your thoughts. In reality, it's not this easy, especially in the beginning. It takes time and energy to change your thoughts. You also need to remain mindful, so you can catch the negative thoughts and focus on techniques to help you change your pattern. For example, you're working on a new project for your supervisor. You want to advance in your career, so the project is more challenging than your previous projects.

At first, you feel confident and believe that you can accomplish the task without too much problem. But, a couple of days later, you find yourself stuck and tell yourself, "I can't do this. It's too complicated." You immediately stop this negative pattern and take a different look at your project. You then switch your thought by saying, "I'll take this step from a different angle." Immediately, you start to feel your confidence coming back as your anxiety diminishes. However, the next day you find yourself still struggling with the project and back to thinking about your negative thoughts. You try to switch to positive thinking, but it doesn't give you the same amount of confidence it did the previous day. Soon, you feel that you're trying to force yourself to think positively.

Switching from negative to positive thought patterns can help decrease your anxiety, give you more confidence, and calm you down. But at the same time, it can lead you into a rut. You can begin to struggle to think positively and then feel that there's no point because the positive thoughts don't stay. This is when positive thinking goes wrong.

Most people don't understand that it takes more than switching your thoughts to change your thought pattern truly. There are many factors that the advice of positive thinking fails to consider or explain to you. First, the culture of positivity has turned into a set of stickers, daily affirmation books, bumper stickers, memes, and quotes that are great to help remind you to stay positive, but they can't do the work for you. Think of the culture as a technique that enables you to maintain a positive mindset. You need to put forth the effort to change your thinking pattern with the aid of this technique.

Second, everyone will react differently to the culture. For example, you might feel that waking up to an affirmation quote helps set the tone for your day while your friend needs to read a few motivational memes near the end of the workday so they can continue working on their project. There are also people who don't believe that you need to write in a gratitude journal while others crave this part of their day.

Positive thinking doesn't work as an on-off switch because it can leave you feeling fake. You feel like you're fooling yourself into thinking a certain way. You might also feel like you're trying to force yourself into thinking positively. This can leave you feeling frustrated, which brings negative thinking right after a positive thought.

Unrealistic expectations cause you to feel like a failure. You become optimistic when you have a happy thought or imagine a situation going a certain way. When the outcome doesn't give you what you wanted, you start to doubt yourself. Furthermore, fantasizing about happy outcomes, while it does calm you down, can drain you of energy. It also fools your mind into perceiving that you've already attained your goal, leading to a lack of motivation to keep working toward your goal.

You can also use positivity as a coping mechanism or a way to ignore the hard truths. A coping mechanism is a strategy you use when faced with stress, so you don't need to deal with the difficult or painful emotion. For example, you lower your expectations, so you're less likely to fail. You might also ask other people to help you with a project because it creates a wall of protection if you make a mistake or miss the deadline.

Another way you can use the cult of positivity as a coping mechanism is by ignoring your negative emotions. Even though it's painful, it's healthy to feel all your feelings, including sadness, anger, and frustration. Emotions play a crucial role in helping you understand how you react to words or situations so you can gain better control of your behavior.

Positive thinking can also lead to delusions. It's amazing what you can imagine. For example, you're sitting at your desk at work and start daydreaming about the mansion you buy once you become a manager. You think about all the vacations you'll take and how you'll never have to worry about money. You start to feel like you'll live the lifestyle of the rich and famous. You receive the manager promotion, but find that the position only pays $10,000 a year more than what you made previously. You become frustrated and feel like you'll never reach your dreams because you allowed your daydreaming to extend beyond reality. You know the raise is a lot, especially for a year, but you still can't purchase the home you dreamed about or go on all the vacations you want.

Ultimately, when you follow the positivity cult, you're missing the process that makes these thoughts work. You're missing a whole range of experiences that you need to help create a better method of thinking. They're useful and legitimate experiences, such as using self-doubt as a motivator to work harder than someone else. Instead of letting yourself become delusional with positive thinking, you need to be realistic. You have to aim for useful and accurate thoughts, so you continue to believe in its true power and not become disappointed by the delusions.

## WHAT SHOULD YOU REALLY DO?

Well, you shouldn't throw your book of affirmations away or stop looking at motivational memes in the morning. Psychologically, these steps can still help your mind move into a calmer direction. But you can't depend on them. You also need to take other steps so you can continue to grow into a positive lifestyle instead of assuming it will move into your life and never leave. You always need to work toward the lifestyle you desire.

One step to take is not to run away from your negative thoughts. You don't want to distract yourself from them either, which is what you feel like you need to do from the memes, quotes, and affirmations you read. Instead, you must defuse them. It's important to acknowledge the negativity and ask yourself, "Why do I think this way?" Take a step back and analyze what you did before the thought popped into your head. Were you working on a project and becoming frustrated? Did you have a flashback to a time when someone criticized you for something you did or said?

You need to distance yourself from the negative thought, once you understand why it came into your mind. For example, if you're studying for an exam and thought, "It doesn't matter how much I'm going to study, I'll still fail," tell yourself, "I am having this thought because of my anxiety." Now that you understand why you told yourself you would fail, you need to switch your thought into a realistic and positive direction. Don't tell yourself, "I will ace the exam." Instead, say, "I believe that I'll do well on the exam because I'm studying."

Another step is to challenge your thoughts. This is when you'll write down evidence for whether it's true or false. Then, you want to analyze your evidence and come up with more accurate and helpful thoughts.

Accepting what you can and cannot control is another way to start changing your method of thinking. In fact, one of the reasons many people struggle with anxiety and negativity is because they focus on what they can't control. You want your family and friends to be happy. You have imagined this caring and peaceful world, but you don't always see this when you look around. Therefore, you want to do what you can to change what's happening around you, but you can't because you can't control someone else's actions. This can make you feel frustrated, angry, and hurt. You put the responsibility on yourself that isn't yours and let it affect your thoughts. You need to understand that you can only control one person—you. Once you give yourself a little less control, you'll start to feel more empowered over what you can control. In response, you stop trying to force other people to be happy and positive and focus on yourself.

You also want to map out the source of your thinking. For example, ask yourself why you continue to follow this thought pattern? Do you feel that you have a flaw that keeps you from thinking positively? Then look for solutions to overcome the negative source so you can focus on the greener side.

Sometimes, the best step you can take is to laugh at your negative thoughts. That's right; take away some of its power. For example, you can say it in a silly voice or giggle and tell yourself, "Oh, sometimes, my mind has a mind of its own." Say or do something that helps you get a little chuckle from the negativity.

One of my dear friends tells the story of when she was in the grocery store, going through her shopping list. "Let's see, I need some rice, milk, lettuce…" she said out loud to herself. Once she realized she was talking out loud to herself, she says she felt kind of stupid. Again, out loud, she said to herself, "Jeez, I talk to myself too much."

Just then, she realized her negative self-talk, and laughed, seeing the genuine humor in it. When we can look at ourselves, and see the humor in what we do, mistakes we make, silly "trip-ups," we can see more positivity.

Focusing on your values over your way of thinking can also help. When negative emotions come into mind, your values can find themselves on the back burner. This doesn't mean that you begin to ignore your values; it just means that your mind is overruling your heart, which is their home. This allows you to become bigger than the negativity. It gives you power over it because it reminds you of what matters the most.

Another quick tip is to know when it's time to push the positivity to the side for a little bit. Yes, sometimes, it is healthier to think more negatively, but only to a certain degree. The truth is, while bold optimism is an excellent characteristic to have, even the most positive people have negative thoughts. You don't want to get rid of them. You just want to control them, so they don't control your life. When you know that negativity is okay in certain instances, you'll manage positive thinking better, and you won't fall into the delusional trap.

For example, let's say you're a manager at a local retail store and push your staff to think positively, even when they come in contact with negative and difficult customers. For months, you've been giving them as much inspiration as possible, but now you're starting to notice that team morale is down. Your employees aren't motivated like they were a few months ago. What's worse is your customers are beginning to see a more depressing environment. You take a couple of steps back and reflect on the last few months. It's at this moment you start to realize the mistakes made and take action to acknowledge them.

During a team meeting, you talk to your employees about how positivity is empowering, but managing their negative thoughts and emotions. You tell them that everyone makes mistakes, and the best step is to realize what they did wrong, learn from it, and move on. You explain the importance of realistic positive thinking and how this is more effective than what you were encouraging them to do before. It's at this moment you acknowledge your own mistakes. After the meeting, you notice morale is already improving, and it continues to increase over the next few weeks.

Another step is to remember that it's okay to feel fear, anxiety, worry, anger, or sadness. It's okay to have these troubling thoughts that the memes tell you not to have. It's a part of life, and sometimes you can't make them go away. This doesn't mean that you can't have realistic, hopeful, optimistic thoughts too. In fact, having a blend of positive and negative is just the way we should sometimes be. You can't always stop the bad parts of life from happening, so you need to make the best out of every situation.

You also want to create active thinking. The more you act on a thought, the more positive you will become. When you simply think "happy thoughts" without realistic action, you're going to become frustrated because you can't reach your delusions. When this happens, you'll begin to go back to the negative thoughts. You'll wonder why you need to put in extra effort to think positively when you always find yourself back at square one.

Take a moment to stop and think about what you're about to say or do. Your choice of words can have an impact on your direction for your life, along with affecting other people. Therefore, choose them carefully. The same goes for your actions. Do your best not to act out in anger or frustration. Take a few steps back and try to stay calm so you can start to think with a clearer mind.

One of the most important steps you can make to bring calmer thinking into your mind is to create a plan of action. You should establish this plan through a series of steps that you will take throughout the day. For example, you decide to wake up with a motivational thought, so you think about what you will do throughout the day to help yourself or someone else. Will you choose to focus on boosting your self-esteem? You might decide to show other people more compassion—including yourself.

Another step is to check in with yourself throughout the day. Set aside time, such as during breaks at work, when you ask yourself how you're doing on your mission for the day. Have you given someone a reason to smile? Have you talked to your-self in a compassionate manner? Have you had negative thoughts? One of the keys to this plan is to be gentle with yourself. If you notice a time when negativity creeps into your mind, accept it and think about how you can change it. If you can't reflect on the thought at that moment, take time to do so later so you can understand where it came from and why.

Other steps that you can incorporate into your plan are identifying areas of change, remaining open to humor, surrounding yourself with positive people, following a healthy lifestyle, and practicing positive self-talk. Through reflection, you might realize that certain parts of your day bring about more negativity than others, such as when you're at work. Think about how you can change this. Do you need to look for a different job or find more self-confidence with your career? If you're a sensitive person, you might struggle to understand the humor in other people. Try not to take everything said personally, especially if you know that the person is joking. Reflect on the people you spend time with. Do you usually carry harmful thoughts? Who could you spend time with that will help you focus on the positive? What foods do you put into your body, and how do they make you feel?

How do you put positive thoughts into practice? Besides following your action plan, you notice your negative thinking and change it to a positive thought. The more you do this, the more it becomes a habit. For example, instead of thinking, "I've never had to do this before," think, "This gives me an opportunity to learn something new." When you think, "There is no way I can make this work," think to yourself, "I can try to make this work." When you bring positive thinking into your life in this manner, you're not ignoring the thought you had; you're focusing on it in a different manner.

You want to become hyper-aware of yourself and everything around you. For example, notice your heartbeat, when you blink, or how your hair feels in your hands. What objects are around you at this moment? If you're sitting on your couch, what is to the left of you and the right? You can touch these objects to notice how they feel, such as rough or smooth. Take a moment to see who else is around you, and if you notice anything about their facial expressions. For instance, are they smiling and happy, or do they look deep in thought?

# 3

# THE POWER OF MINDFULNESS

---

*"When we get too caught up in the busyness of the world, we lose connection with one another – and ourselves."*

— JACK KORNFIELD (SELVA, 2019)

---

You know that you can have negative or positive thoughts. But you can also be mindful or mindless when it comes to your thinking. Mindlessness is when you're going through the motions. You're not directly aware of what you're doing. You tend to get lost in your thoughts and forget what's going on around you. For example, you're driving the same road to work as every other day. You've seen the sights thousands of times, so you don't think about the drive, landmarks, or anything else in front of you. Instead, you turn on the music, start singing, and then realize that you're about two minutes away from work, but you can't remember going through a town, passing the river, or most of the drive.

The challenge with mindlessness is that it's easy for you to sink into this mindset because your brain is wired this way. But this doesn't mean that you can't train yourself and your brain to become more mindful. While you can't always be mindful, you can teach yourself to notice certain thoughts and use tricks and tips to help bump your brain into mindfulness throughout the day.

Mindfulness is the ability to remain fully present for a period of time. It helps build awareness of how you think. It helps you notice where you are, what you are doing, how you feel, and how you're reacting or are about to react. It can help you remain calm in a stressful situation and keep you from overreacting. It can also help keep you safe because it makes you aware of what other people are doing around you.

Mindfulness helps bring awareness to your thoughts because it makes you realize that they're nothing more than thoughts. You understand what you're doing in the present moment without forming any judgment. Even though you're more likely to think on a mindless level, mindfulness is available to you throughout your day. It doesn't matter if you're meditating, listening to music, working, or watching television. By taking time to pause and breathe, you can regain control of your thoughts.

For example, when you're making dinner, reflect on the smells and how the food combines as it cooks. Notice how the texture and smell changes during the cooking process. Before you take action, think about what you're doing. For instance, if you're grabbing the plates to set the table, think about what hand you use to open the cupboard door and how you reach for the dishes. How do they feel when you grab them? Do they become heavy? Are they light and plastic? Do you feel the rims along the side of the plate?

## THE SCIENCE OF MINDFULNESS

Researchers have looked at the science behind mindfulness for years.

One study conducted at the University of Mexico showed that participants who took a Mindfulness-Based Stress Reduction course and used those strategies to de-stress had decreased signs of anxiety, depression, and eating disorders. Other studies have used the same stress reduction course. Their participants improved their immune system function, lowered levels of drug use, exhibited better self-control, and showed improvement in emotional, physical, and mental health. Many participants even felt less stress and anxiety about their weight (Siegel, 2010).

Science still doesn't know precisely how the brain works, but they do know that mindfulness changes how the brain functions. This starts to happen because increasing mindfulness activates many areas in the neocortex, which is the layer that covers the cerebral hemisphere (Keane, 2018). In total, there are six layers in the neocortex, and mindfulness will activate the bottom two layers. This is a large part of the human brain, which is in charge of many complex functions, such as conscious thought, language, social control, and abstract thinking.

The longer you practice mindfulness, the more your brain's function will change. In the long-term, you'll enhance behavioral activation and extroversion instead of showing behaviors of inhibition. This happens because your left frontal and prefrontal areas become more activated than the right. By activating this part of the brain, you drive yourself more toward social behaviors, and it becomes easier to come up with potential solutions to problems.

It's also known that there are changes in brain structure, specifically, integration of specific brain areas that are key to emotional regulation, memory, and learning. On the basis, this means that you're more in control of your emotions, thoughts, and behaviors. Scientifically, this happens because the neocortex increases in thickness.

In particular, all the changes in the brain structure and their areas of focus include:

- Insular cortex - empathy, crying, pain, and laughter
- Hippocampus - memory
- Prefrontal cortex - social control, planning, inhibiting responses, planning, and language
- Posterior cingulate gyrus - memory and emotion
- Cerebellum - balance, speech, posture, coordination
- Temporo-parietal junction - empathy, attention, and language

Scientists understand the ways mindfulness changes the brain because of MRI scans and dozens of studies. Many of these studies are combined to support each other and give researchers a more accurate representation of mindfulness. It also helps them understand the benefits of mindfulness and how it works to ensure the improvement of your overall health.

## BENEFITS OF MINDFULNESS

There are several benefits of mindfulness. Some of them you'll start to feel immediately after you begin practicing, while other benefits you'll notice as time goes on. This will allow you to notice the changes over a period of time; they tend to happen gradually, making it hard to realize what is happening to your mind, body, mental, emotional, and physical health. A journal will help you understand how you've grown and improved in your life by using mindfulness techniques like we'll be talking more about in this book.

Mindfulness also improves your memory and is even linked to decreasing your chances of certain brain disorders, such as Alzheimer's disease and dementia (Suttie, 2018). When you remain mindful, you slow your cognitive decline because you're improving working memory and becoming more cognitively flexible. Blood flow to the brain increases; this not only improves your concentration, but it also leads to a stronger network of blood vessels (O'Connor, 2019). This reinforces the capacity of your memory so you can store more information in your memory bank.

Your memory also improves because you train your mind to limit distractions. Instead of feeling that you're being pulled 20 different directions, you can focus on what you need. Researchers at Harvard conducted a study that focused on an eight-week mindfulness training program. They focused on how well the participants focused on a task throughout the eight weeks. Researchers also looked at the habits that participants established as a result of the program. The researchers concluded that participants who used mindfulness techniques followed the training program and incorporated productive habits improved their memory. Participants weren't affected by as many distractions at the end of the program, compared to the beginning. They felt that they could "tune out" the distractions because they were more focused on their task (Cho, 2016).

Another benefit is that your relationships will improve. You feel that you can connect better with people because you can understand them better. You become more aware of their feelings and yours. This allows you to address a negative situation in a thorough way. For instance, if you notice your coworker becoming irritated, you can understand that they're reacting this way due to frustration they feel from their project and not that you came to ask them a question. You also understand that humans are all connected, and this makes you feel closer to people.

Several studies have proven that mindfulness lowers stress. One reason is that you start to feel calm and relaxed, even in times of stress. You might simply think that you don't have much to worry about because "everything will work out as it needs to." Mindfulness helps you learn coping strategies when it comes to stress. For example, you learn how to control your emotion, so you don't overthink a situation, as this usually leads to stress.

Another reason why mindfulness decreases stress is that it simply puts you in a better mood. You're more mindful of your health, so you focus on what you're eating, the amount of sleep you get, and exercise more. This helps you feel better emotionally, physically, and mentally. In return, your body starts to feel less stressed because you have more energy to regulate your emotions and thoughts. This helps keep your stress levels under control.

One of the best parts about learning mindfulness is you gain the power to familiarize yourself with thoughts and patterns. You start to understand and get to know your critical inner voice. You'll begin to notice your destructive thoughts of labeling and self-doubt when they surface. You can then take the time to choose your thoughts, steering them in a positive direction.

Mindfulness helps focus your mind and reduces brain clutter. Do you ever feel that your mind is going 100 miles per hour, and you can't seem to form one thought? It makes you feel like your mind is on overload, and you can't focus on your task at hand. This is more common than you think and is often the cause of stress and overthinking. When you start to feel this way, it's time to turn to mindfulness because it helps train your mind to focus on what is important. You'll learn to allow the thoughts that are cluttering your mind to leave, giving your important thoughts more room to stretch out. This helps you feel more relaxed, which further increases your ability to concentrate.

When you become mindful, your creativity also gets a boost. Part of this is because you're thinking more clearly and have more energy, in general. Your mind easily switches to divergent thinking (problem-solving by exploring many possible solutions or ideas), which is one of the essential skills necessary for creative problem-solving. This leaves you open to new ideas. Another essential skill that opens up is your attentiveness, which helps you foster innovative ideas. Finally, you become more courageous and resilient, even when you're faced with setbacks. This is an essential part because you'll face criticism during the creative process.

Through mindfulness, you'll tend to have less emotional reactivity. You don't respond to situations drastically because you remain aware of your emotions and thoughts. You think about how what you do or say will affect other people and yourself. For example, you're in the middle of a disagreement with your partner, and the longer it goes on, the angrier you become. Soon, you find yourself lashing out at your partner and opening old wounds. You yell at them because you're not only hurt by the present disagreement but also what happened in the past. When you react this way, your partner becomes just as angry and starts to lash out at you. In response, you find yourself overwhelmed and leave the house without taking the time to calm down to settle the argument.

The above situation is a common theme in relationships, and one reason why many fail. When you practice mindfulness, you become more aware of how you're acting, and you realize that what you say and do can and does have an effect on your partner. You understand that your partner is choosing to act in an emotional way because you're acting the same. You realize that you're not upset with your partner, you're frustrated by the lack of communication between you. When you practice mindfulness, you're better able to control your outbursts, which helps you improve your relationship satisfaction.

## TUNING INTO MINDFULNESS DURING YOUR DAY

When you're starting to practice mindfulness, you need to follow a certain process for it to work effectively.

*Observe the present moment.* When you feel like you've been mindless, begin observing the present moment. No matter what you're doing, start thinking about your actions, words, and thoughts. For example, if you're eating dinner with your family, notice what is being said by everyone, how they tell their words, and what food is on their plate. Observe the foods they eat first, how quickly or slowly they eat and then focus on your own eating. How many times do you chew your food? Take time to notice the smell as the food comes closer to your mouth. Take notice of the texture and look of your food.

The key to observing the present moment is the aim of mindfulness. You don't need to make sure that your mind is quiet or that you feel calm. What you need to do is keep your mind in the present. Don't think about any past mistakes or what you need to do in the future. Just focus on what is going on at that moment.

*Let your judgments roll on.* No matter how hard you try, judgments enter your mind. You will judge yourself along with other people. These thoughts can often cling to you. You overthink the decision you made and wonder why you think in such away. The truth is, you're not the only one who has thoughts like this. Everyone does. The key is to recognize the thought and then let it leave your mind. Don't continue to focus on it because this will bring up more negative emotions and thoughts.

*Return to observing the present moment* as it is. Once you start to notice your judgments, take a moment to bring yourself back into the present.

But there are times when you want to focus on clearing your mind from any thoughts. You want to allow the calmness of the environment to enter your mind; this is a challenge when your thoughts are rushing through your mind like speeding cars. While you want to focus on releasing your thoughts, you don't want to become irritated by them.

When you allow negative feelings to enter, your thoughts will become negative. You'll start to become frustrated with the mindfulness process and feel that it doesn't work for you. You might find yourself giving up. But, when you're kind to the thoughts that wander in, you simply acknowledge them, and then gently bring your mind back to its peaceful state; you'll feel more content and calm. You may feel like you can accomplish anything you set your mind to during your day.

One of the best courses of action to take is to savor the process. It doesn't matter if you're drinking your morning coffee, trying to get your children to get dressed and eating their breakfast, or making dinner after a hectic day. Slow down and pay attention to the small details in your actions to help you stay mindful.

*Remember to move.* While you can take time to put your feet up and relax, you don't want to spend too much time lying down or sitting. Get up and do some exercise, whether this is going for a walk or doing yoga. Keeping active will not only help you sleep at night, but it can help you practice mindfulness as you pay close attention to details within your exercises. For example, count the number of steps you take in a minute or notice your toes every time they touch the concrete. How does your body feel when you practice certain yoga poses, for example?

*Regular meditations will sharpen your daily mindfulness skills.* You will quickly learn that practicing mindfulness every day is more challenging than you thought. Even though the process is simple, it doesn't take away the fact that your mind likes to do what it's always done, and that is to overwhelm you with various thoughts, even when you're trying to focus. The trick is to continue to practice every day, even several times a day. The more you continue to practice, the more you'll notice results.

## MINDFUL MEDITATION

Mindful meditation is the best way to sharpen your mindfulness skills. Doing this every day allows you to gradually cultivate more awareness and be less caught up in your mind. It's backed by several studies that show ways in which mindful meditation is beneficial to your brain.

One study conducted by the University of California, Los Angeles (UCLA) studied mindful meditation. They concluded that participants who meditated regularly preserved their brains better than people who didn't meditate. The study showed that people who meditated for nearly 20 years had more gray matter than participants who didn't meditate. The brain's gray matter tends to decrease as we age, causing a lot of memory loss and mental diseases such as Alzheimer's (Walton, 2015). By meditating regularly, whether it's every day or a few days a week, you can help preserve your aging brain.

Another study done by Yale University researchers shows that mindfulness meditation decreases activity in the brain's "me center." This is the area known as the default mode network (DMN) and is responsible for the area of self-referential thoughts or wandering thoughts. This part of the brain is switched on when you're mindless or not focused on your thoughts. While this isn't necessarily bad, psychologically mindlessness is associated with more unhappy thoughts, worrying about the past, or having anxiety about the present and future. This study shows that meditation can help you stay focused on the present, which is associated with feeling happier and less stressed.

Jon Kabat-Zinn from the University of Massachusetts' Center

for Mindfulness developed the Mindfulness-Based Stress Reduction (MBSR), which focuses on how mindfulness strategies decrease the amount of stress you feel on a daily basis. They have done several studies to prove that this course provides positive results in reducing your stress level. One study showed that even years after the course, there are still positive effects. Another study proved that mindful meditation has a more powerful impact on a person than simply following deep breathing exercises. Stress is a constant in your life, and while a certain level is natural, it's easy to become over-stressed, which leads to worry. Through meditation, you can limit the negative emotions, such as stress, and focus on more ways to limit stress.

4

MINDFUL MEDITATION

---

*"The more regularly and the more deeply you meditate, the sooner you will find yourself acting always from a center of peace."*

— J. DONALD WALTERS

---

When you're first getting started with meditation, it's easy to get frustrated. You feel that your mind wanders too much, or you're not sure how to begin. I've included some simple exercises that you can take to help you get started. You'll eventually develop your own routine and "script," but I have some first steps here.

Each guide follows the basic steps for this type of meditation:

1. Find a comfortable and quiet location where you can sit or lay down for several minutes. Set up your area so you can relax and focus on the mediation. For instance, turn off all electronic devices, turn soothing music to a low volume, and/or light a candle.

2. Breathe deeply in through your nose and out through your mouth. Focus on your breath and notice where you breathe deeply the most. Keep your attention on these areas as your mind starts to drift into a meditative state, and your body starts to release any stress.

3. When you start to feel more relaxed, bring your breathing to its normal rhythm. Focus on your slow breaths as you start to scan your body to notice any tension spots. Spend extra time on these areas so you can completely release all of your tension.

4. When you begin bringing yourself out of the meditative state, do so slowly. Start by focusing on your body's sensations; wiggle your toes, fingers, and slowly move your head. Open your eyes and let your mind connect with your home before you sit up and go about your day.

### *Guided Meditation for Breathing Awareness*

You can't perform any meditations without becoming aware of your breathing. This guide will help you focus on your breaths to incorporate breathing awareness into your daily life.

Throughout this meditation, you want to breathe at a slow and steady pace.

> *Find a comfortable spot. To start, breathe in and count to four. Hold your breath to the count of three. Then, breathe out to the count of five.*
>
> *Breathe in 1, 2, 3, 4.*
>
> *Hold your breath 1, 2, 3.*
>
> *Breathe out 1, 2, 3, 4, 5.*
>
> *Keep breathing at this slow and steady pace.*
>
> *When you are breathing, notice how your body feels at different awareness states.*
>
> *Notice your breath as the air flows through your nose and into your body. Become aware of your body's sensation each time you breathe in.*
>
> *Feel how the sensations change as the air goes through your nose and down your throat.*

*Let your breath continue going down into your lungs.*

*How do you feel as the air expands your lungs? What happens to your chest and stomach?*

*Let your awareness become more profound as you start to glide into a state of relaxation.*

*Breathe in, allowing your lungs to expand. Breathe out, allowing your body to relax.*

*Turn your focus to the exhalation phase. Feel the air as it leaves your lungs and travels upward into your throat, mouth, and lips.*

*Breathe in, hold, breathe out. Take each breath as a new whole. Visualize your breath, slowing like calm water waves.*

*Breathe in, hold, breathe out. Continue to count your breaths as they flow through your body and then back out.*

*Count up to 10 breaths. Notice how your muscles begin to feel more relaxed with each passing breath. Observe how regular your breathing has become.*

*Your body is going deeper into a relaxing state. Focus on this emotion until you're ready to return to your day. Start by bringing your body's sensations slowly back into reality. Wiggle your toes, fingers, and stretch out your muscles.*

*Count to five, becoming more alert with each number.*

*1, 2, 3, 4, 5.*

### Guided Meditation for Body Scan

One of the most important steps to learn in guided meditation is how to scan your body. This script will help you learn the basics so you can incorporate it throughout other meditations.

*Take a few deep breaths to begin clearing your mind. Breathe slowly, taking your time with each breath. Allow the feeling of calmness to start filling your mind.*

*Focus on your breathing. Let each breath come*

*at its own pace without any conscious effort.*

*When you focus on this body scan, you'll observe every part of your body passively. You don't want to make any changes or move to cause any type of additional pain. You simply want to notice your body and sensations as your mind moves from one part to the next.*

*Start with your toes. Notice how they feel as you lay in a relaxed position. Take time to notice each toe.*

*Now, move on to your left foot. Take a moment to notice how it feels or if you feel any changes when you focus your attention on it.*

*Next, move to your right foot and follow the same system. If your foot feels tingly or warm, take note.*

*Observe both of your feet together. Do they feel the same? Do they feel different? Do you notice the temperature? Is anything touching your feet?*

*Move your body scan up to your ankles. Notice how they feel.*

*Now, take a moment to breathe in, breathe out. Let your breaths come naturally as you continue to move up to your lower legs. Concentrate on the feeling of your lower legs. Observe them passively.*

*Move up your leg and into your knees. Notice your kneecaps; allow your mind to move into your upper legs. Notice how both of your legs feel together.*

*Continue to move along your body and focus on your hips, now your lower abdomen.*

*Move up to the center of your body. Move into your stomach, chest, lower back, and upper back. Notice how your body feels. Observe the sensations passively. Scan your sides. Notice and observe your body.*

*Now, turn your focus to your fingertips and how they feel.*

*Move up your palms, wrists, arms, into your elbows, shoulders, and your neck. Collectively observe your arms and any sensations.*

*Bring your focus back to your breathing. Let any wandering thoughts escape with each passing breath.*

*Continue up to your neck, jaw, and notice how it feels. Is your jaw relaxed, or does it feel tense?*

*Move up to your cheeks, nose, eyes, forehead, ears, and the top of your head. Passively observe your neck, jaw, and head.*

*Then, mentally scan your body as a whole. Do another complete scan at your own pace. Start with your feet and go all the way up to your head. As you come back through your body, do you notice anything different? Do you feel more relaxed and calmer? Is your jaw, less tense?*

*If you notice any areas that interest you, take time, and focus on them. Notice how your muscles feel and the sensations of your body.*

*Now, it is time to start bringing your mind back into reality. Start by moving your fingers and toes. If your eyes are closed, open them, and scan the room before you begin moving your body. Breathe in and out at your normal pace. Allow yourself to regain energy before you sit up and continue with your day.*

### Guided Meditation for Sleep

The first guided meditation is to increase the amount of sleep you get every night. Sleep is an important step if you want to remain mindful throughout the day. On average, you should get between seven and eight hours of sleep. It helps if you create a relaxing bedtime routine; this includes turning off your phone and television at least thirty minutes prior to going to bed.

*Lay down in your bed and find a comfortable sleeping position. This sleep meditation countdown allows you to move around when you need to but try to keep to one spot.*

*Start by taking a deep breath in, hold it for a
couple of seconds, and then breathe out.
Scan your body, starting at the top of your
head, slowly moving down your face, neck,
shoulders, and the rest of your body. Look
for areas of tension and focus on relaxing
these muscles.*

*As your body starts to relax, let yourself sink
into the bed. Allow your jaw to drop
slightly as your facial muscles relax.*

*Feel the sensations of your body. Wiggle your
toes once. Open and close your hands once
or twice. Let your body continue to sink
into its relaxed state.*

*Turn your attention back to your breath. Let
your natural breath turn into a rhythm.
Breathe in, breathe out, breathe in, breathe
out. Feel the tension in your abdomen and
chest. Now, take a deep breath in through
your nose. Hold this breath as you allow
your lungs to fill with air. Slowly release
the breath through your mouth, letting the
tension from inside you flow out of your
body and into the air where it dissolves.*

*Continue to scan your body, focusing on the areas of tension. Release the stress from your body with each deep breath.*

*Now you will start to countdown to your sleep. Start with the number 50, breathing in slowly and silently. When you breathe in, picture the number in your mind. When you breathe out, allow the number to escape your body.*

*Take a deep breath in and imagine the number 49 in your mind's eye. Release the breath through your mouth and visualize the number flowing out of your body with the air.*

*Now picture the number 48. Breathe in, noticing your eyelids are feeling heavy. Your body is becoming comfortable. Breathe out.*

*See the number 47. Focus your attention on this digit as you exhale.*

*Your body is starting to feel more relaxed. Breathe in. Imagine the number 46.*

*Breathe out.*

45. *Your mind is becoming sleepy.*

44. *Your breathing is slowing down and finding a new rhythm.*

43. *Your mind feels calm.*

42. *Your body is further sinking into the comfort of your bed.*

41. *Your attention is starting to drift slowly toward random thoughts. Gently bring your mind back to the number.*

*Imagine the number 40 in your mind's eye as you take another relaxing breath.*

*As you begin to feel calmer, see the number 39. Release it from your mind.*

38. *Your body is feeling safe in your comfortable bed.*

37. *Your mind is in a peaceful state.*

*36. You're beginning to feel very sleepy now.*

*35. You're pleasantly drifting off into sleep.*

*34. Continue to focus on the numbers. Allow any other thoughts to slip away from your mind.*

*33. You feel deeply relaxed.*

*32. Deeper and deeper into a relaxed state.*

*31. Continue to count down on your own now. Focus on the numbers as your mind starts to drift off into sleep.*

*When your mind begins to wander, bring it back to the numbers.*

*You're pleasantly drifting into sleep.*

*You're calm.*

*Your body is relaxed.*

*You're at peace.*

*Continue to count down all the way to zero,*
*down into a peaceful and relaxed sleep.*

## Guided Meditation for Reducing Anxiety

*Find a comfortable place to lay down. Close*
*your eyes and take a deep breath in*
*through your nose. Release the breath*
*through your mouth and allow your mind*
*to begin to clear.*

*Breathe normally. Breathe in and out. Don't*
*rush your breathing, but let it calm you. As*
*your body starts to relax, take another*
*deep, slow breath through your nose.*
*Exhale out of your mouth. Blow all the air*
*out like you're blowing out a candle.*

*Take another deep breath in. Allow your lungs*
*to fill with air. Release the breath slowly.*
*Inhale again, slowing down your*
*breathing. Exhale fully, allow your breaths*
*to enter a calm rhythm. Continue focusing*
*on your breathing, letting your body sink*
*into a comfortable position. Slowly, calmly,*
*your mind is beginning to reach a peaceful*
*state.*

*Your body now has the oxygen it needs. Let your mind drift to the thoughts that bother you. Focus on them one at the time. Keep your calm and peaceful state as you think about these thoughts. Take a deep, slow breath when you feel the anxiety rise in your body. Your breathing makes you stronger so you can release your worries.*

*Accept your anxious feeling. Mentally tell yourself, "I'm feeling anxiety now, but I know I am okay. I know this feeling will pass. No harm will come to me. Even though I feel afraid, I am safe. I will reach my calm state. I will push through the anxiety I am experiencing right now. I will get through this. I am comfortable. My anxiety is decreasing, flowing out of my body. My mind is becoming calm. I'm drifting into a relaxed state."*

*As you continue to mentally give yourself peaceful messages, breathe in slowly. Fully exhale, releasing the anxiety inside you. With each breath in, you bring calm energy. With each breath out, you release worry and tension.*

*Keep telling yourself calming thoughts as you breathe in, breathe out, breathe in, breathe out.*

*Breathe in; you're becoming more relaxed.*

*Breathe out; the anxiety is leaving your body. You're reaching a calmer state.*

*Breathe in; you're feeling at peace.*

*Breathe out; you're feeling calm.*

*Now, scan your body. Start at the top of your head and work your way down to your toes, slowly. As you move down from your head into your neck, notice any tense muscles. Focus on these anxiety spots and release the worry and stress when you exhale. Relax your jaw and continue to scan your body. Relax your shoulders, back, arms, torso, and legs. When you reach your feet, wiggle your toes. Let all the anxiety escape with each movement of your toes.*

*Your body feels limp. You're relaxed and calm.*

*Move and stretch your muscles, releasing any leftover tension.*

*Breathe in, breathe out. Let your mind come back to your breathing. Continue to focus on your breath until you feel completely relaxed, calm.*

### Guided Meditation for Self-Compassion

This is a short meditation break that you can use anytime when you need to add a little self-compassion into your day.

*Start by finding a place you can begin to relax your mind and body. Take a deep breath in through your nose and then release it with your mouth. Take another deep but slower breath in, allowing the air to fill your lungs. Slowly exhale out of your mouth like you're blowing out a candle.*

*Now breathe in and out normally. Find a rhythm in your breath that you can focus on. Allow yourself to become more relaxed as you focus on your calm breathing. Take a moment to realize that this is a moment of suffering. Take a moment to use language that speaks to you about the difficult situation in your mind, like "This is hard right now" or "I'm struggling with this." Acknowledge your struggle. Give it a name.*

*Continue to breathe in, breathe out. Take your mind back to your regular breathing that helps you feel more at peace. Tell yourself that suffering is a part of life. It's a part of humanity. Use your words to explain that many people feel this way. Other people go through similar situations. The degree might be different, but suffering is a part of life.*

*Turn back to your breathing. Slowly breathe in, breathe out. Turn your thought to a phrase that reminds you to be kind to yourself. Place your hand on your heart or another part of your body that feels comforting. Notice your gentle touch and the warmth of your hands. Imagine our feelings of self-compassion flow through your fingers. Find your own language that supports kindness toward yourself. Say something that you would tell your friend going through a similar situation. You* might say, "I'm sorry you're going through this."

Bring your mind back to your breathing. Start bringing yourself out of the meditative practice by feeling the sensations of your body. Wiggle your toes and fingers. Gently move other parts of your body. If you closed your eyes, open them, and slowly start to bring yourself back into your day, remembering the kind words you told yourself.

## Guided Meditation for Healing

Find a comfortable position.

Start by focusing on your breathing. Take a normal breath in, breathe out. Let your body start sinking into a relaxing state.

Breathe in, breathe out. Take a deep, cleansing breath in through your nose. Once your lungs fill with air, release the breath. Allow the tension in your body to start flowing out with the air.

*Feel a relaxing sensation come into your body through the bottom of your feet. Notice how your feet feel like they've stepped into a nice, warm bubbly bathtub. The muscles in your feet are feeling loose as the tension begins to dissolve.*

*Let the relaxing sensation move up toward your ankles. They start to tingle as the feeling continues to move up into your legs. If you feel any pain inside your body, focus on these areas before the relaxation continues to move up your body.*

*Allow the feeling to move into your thighs, hips, and lower back. Take a moment to focus on this area as you feel the warm tingly sensation place a calm blanket over your body. Move further up your back, into your stomach, chest, and into your neck. Release the muscles of your jaw as they relax.*

*Let the feeling move into your shoulder blades. Feel them sink into a comfortable position as they relax. The sensation continues to spread down your arms and into your*

*hands, releasing any pain through your
fingers.*

*Move your focus back to your neck and let
your relaxation move through your cheeks,
eyes, forehead, and to the top of your head.
Once the sensation reaches the top of your
head, visualize all your pain, leaving your
body. It dissolves and goes out through
your toes, fingertips, head, and breath.*

*Feel your body continue to relax as you sink
into complete calmness and peacefulness.
Your eyelids are becoming heavy, relaxing
with your mind and body.*

*Your whole body is now calm and relaxed. It's
flowing through your veins; your muscles
continue to become heavy as your body
sinks further into relaxation.*

*Take another deep relaxing breath in. Release
the breath and all the remaining tension in
your body.*

*Bring your breathing back to a relaxing
rhythm and slowly scan your body,*

*starting at the top of your head. When you
notice any remaining tension, pay
attention to that area. Bring the relaxing
sensation into that area so it can dissolve
the tension, releasing it from your body.*

*Now bring your attention back to your
breathing. Breathe in, breathe out. Find
your calm and peaceful rhythm and allow
this feeling to fill your body.*

*Imagine your current state of being. Think
about an ailment that bothers you, whether
illness, pain, or injury. Maybe you don't
know or understand what you're feeling;
you know you're struggling and want to
heal this problem.*

*Focus on the issue and imagine it as a dark
area. Picture a healing white light flowing
through your body and toward the
darkness. As the light moves closer, it
becomes brighter. Slowly the darkness
turns into the white healing light.*

*Your body is healing. You're feeling stronger as
your immune system heals. Any unhealthy*

*matter is dissolving, and healthy tissue is growing in your body. The waste and toxins are leaving as this white light is cleaning up your body.*

*Visualize the light circling any remaining darkness, breaking it up into pieces, and carrying them out of your body as you breathe out.*

*Breathe in healing, calm energy.*

*Breathe out darkness, tension, and illness.*

*Breathe in the light that soothes your body.*

*Breathe out any problems that you feel.*

*As the light continues to flow in your body, imagine the darkness completely gone. You're now filled with healing light and energy.*

*Continue to breathe normally as you start bringing yourself back to alertness. One, you're starting to hear the noises and smell the aroma around you. Two, you begin to wiggle your toes and fingers. Three, you now open your eyes and scan the room before you continue with your day.*

## Guided Meditation for Relaxation

*Find a comfortable location and lay down. Close your eyes. Take a couple of minutes to relax your mind and body.*

*Start by placing one hand on your chest and the other on your stomach. Take a few deep, slow breaths. Every time you breathe in, slowly breath through your nose. Breathe in all the way down into your stomach. Notice how your lungs and abdomen fill with air. Feel your stomach and chest expand as you breathe in deeply. Slowly exhale and allow your breath to flow through your mouth and out of your body. With each breath, let go of the stress in your body. Feel your muscles begin to relax as your body releases the tension you held on to. As you continue to breathe, mentally say the word "relax" with each releasing breath.*

*Continue breathing deeply and slowly. Don't rush your breath. Let your lungs fill with air and then release that breath completely. Breathe in, breathe out, breathe in, breathe out. You're beginning to feel yourself relaxing. Each breath dissolves your stress like warm water melting ice.*

*Breathe in, breathe out. Breathe in and feel your body fill with air. Once you are ready, release that breath, allowing it to flow naturally out of your lungs and body. Breathe in, breathe out. Breathe in deeply, slowly. Your mind is relaxing. Your muscles are relaxing. Your arms might slide down to your sides as they relax. Gradually release the last breath completely out of your lungs, through your mouth, and out into the air.*

*Relax your breathing into its normal rhythm. Breathe in, breathe out, breathe in, breathe out. Feel the quiet, soft beating of your heart as it connects to the rhythm of your breath. It's time to scan your entire body, from your toes to your head. Look for areas of tension to release. Move through your body, focusing on each part one by one. Feel your toes and move into your feet. Bring your awareness into your angels, and slowly move up your leg and into your kneecap. Feel the relaxing sensation overcome your legs as you release the tension.*

*Keep moving up your legs, into your thighs, hips, and then lower back. Stop and focus on your back as the relaxing sensation takes over, releasing the stress. Imagine this sensation moving into your abdomen, up to your chest, back, and neck. Focus your attention on your neck muscles that connect to your jaw, shoulders, and arms. Feel your shoulders go with the release of tension. Mentally soothe these muscles, allowing them to relax. Feel the muscles loosen as they let go of the tension.*

*Let the relaxing sensation glide into the muscles in your face. Your cheeks and forehead relax. Your eye muscles feel at peace as the tension slowly dissolves away. Let the muscles in your body continue to*

*relax with your slow breath. Let your*
*mind rest with the sensation of your body.*

*Now bring your attention back to your*
*stomach as it gently rises and falls with*
*each breath. Allow these breaths to release*
*the rest of the tension in your body. Feel*
*the way your mind and body slowly slip*
*into a state of deep relaxation. Stay in*
*that state for a couple of minutes, focusing*
*on your breaths. Breathe in and breathe*
*out.*

*Slowly bring your mind back into the*
*sensation of your body. Wiggle your toes*
*and fingers, and you begin to awake from*
*your meditative state. Open your eyes and*
*allow your mind and body to come back*
*into the physical world. Once you're ready,*
*slowly get up and continue with your day.*

## TIPS TO HELP WITH MEDITATION

Learning to meditate takes some doing. It is difficult to just start
practicing and learning it on your own. You may feel intimi-
dated to go to a class, and a class might not be enough by itself.
Becoming a monk seems to be a bit extreme for most of us.

Having guided meditations is a great way to start learning and practicing.

## So, where do you find help with that?

Well, of course, these days, there is an app for that. Actually, there are many apps to help you. They all offer the same variety of meditations: for beginners, anxiety, sleep, mindful, etc. I have found with any guided meditation, the essential factor is the voice and the narrator's pace. Use the one with the voice that most resonates with you and is the most soothing to you.

Here is a brief rundown of a few of the top apps out there:

## Headspace

I really like Headspace's interface with its unique cartoon characters. Headspace is broken down into five sections; Today, Meditate, Sleep, Move, and Focus.

1. TODAY – Here is a daily inspirational or educational video.
2. MEDITATE – This, of course, includes a wide variety of meditations, but also courses, timers, and tips. Another thing that makes Headspace different is that within each meditation, you are able to select your timeframe; 3, 5, 10, 20 minutes. There is also a section for group meditations.
3. SLEEP – Here is where you will find relaxing music to help you fall asleep.

4. MOVE – Exercises to help you move and stretch.
5. FOCUS – To help you focus, they offer; Music, Exercises, and Sounds.

They also offer a free trial version for two weeks. If you decide to keep it, you need to pay $69.99 annually (which equals $5.83/month). You also have the choice of trying it for one free week and then paying monthly at $12.99 (Headspace Inc, 2012).

## CALM

This app is loaded with hundreds of guided meditations ranging from 3 to 30 minutes. Calm is broken down into four sections; Sleep, Meditate, Music, and More.

1. SLEEP – Here, you find soothing bedtime stories and meditations, including ones for Kids. The list of offers includes; fiction, non-fiction, music, nature, soundscapes, and more. Many of the stories are professionally narrated by some famous people.
2. MEDITATE – Here, you will find a vast selection of meditations broken down into several categories; anxiety, beginners, stress, work, self-care, inner peace, focus, emotions, less guidance, relationships, personal growth, kids and guest instructors.
3. MUSIC – Music includes; sleep, soundscapes, nature, work, relax, lullabies, and focus.
4. MORE – The main features of this section include

Calm Masterclass, which are workshops that will continue your education with mindfulness and more. Also, here you will find Calm Body, which is not just exercises but exercises focusing on mindfulness. This will help improve your mindfulness practice and show how it can be applied to anything you do.

This app is free to download with some meditations and feature that you can try, you then need to pay for the premium version. You can get a 7-day free trial; then, it's $47.99/year. (Calm, 2014).

## INSIGHT TIMER

Insight Timer has a library of over 35,000 free meditations (Insight Network, Inc, 2020). This app allows you to listen to a number of meditation musicians and teachers, such as the Emeritus Professor at Oxford University, Mark Williams, and the founder of Insight Meditation Community of Washington, Tara Brach. You can also join many community groups that focus on what you want to accomplish or your beliefs, such as poetry, Hinduism, Christianity, and beginners. You can purchase the premium feature for $59.99/year ("Insight Timer - Meditation App," n.d.). The premium feature will give you access to over 400 courses.

There are many other features of these apps. This is just a brief overview. Do you need to pay for an app to get into the habit of meditating successfully? Absolutely not. However, all of the above apps are of high quality and offer much more than just guided meditation. If they help get you to start with a habit of meditation and mindfulness, then the money spent is absolutely worth it. Download them, give them a try, and see what works for you.

One tip to give you the best meditation experience possible is to meditate for only a few minutes a day. Most of the guided meditations listed above are short, between 10 to 20 minutes long. With practice, some people meditate longer 30 minutes or more, but you don't need to strive for this lofty goal to gain the benefits. Aiming for 10 to 15 minutes is fine. While many studies have looked at a magic number, no set time frame will give you the best experience. You simply have to go with what you feel is best for you, whether that's 5 or 30 minutes. However, what the studies have shown is that people benefit more from short bursts than longer ones.

Consistency is one of the most important factors when you're meditating. You want to commit to focusing on a certain time every day, whether in the morning or before you go to bed. You can use many strategies to maintain consistency, such as focusing on one goal at the time. Ask yourself, "What do I want to achieve from meditating?" Making it a part of your daily routine will help you turn into a habit, but it's essential to make yourself accountable.

Find time to fit meditation into your week by adding it into your schedule or your phone, so you get a notification when it's time to meditate. You can also ask your partner or a friend to help keep you on schedule as they'll motivate you to continue. It's also important to have one location, such as your couch or a unique area of your home that you decorate for your meditation practice. However, you shouldn't worry if you can't create a designated space for meditation. If you need to get a little creative, such as going for a walk or meditating during a break at work, go for it.

You'll want to make sure that you're comfortable, so find the best position for you. If you don't like sitting with your legs crossed, don't do it. You might feel that lying down or having your feet flat on the floor helps maintain your focus. Make sure that your limbs won't fall asleep or won't feel any, body aches from lying or sitting a certain way. Once you start meditating, you'll want to maintain this position until you're done; if you're uncomfortable, you might end the meditation earlier or find yourself focusing on your pain.

Another tip is to choose to forgive yourself repeatedly. There will be days that you can't meditate for many reasons. When you focus on a negative event, your thought pattern can become negative. For example, when you're meditating, and you notice your mind starting to wander, forgive yourself. Don't get frustrated because you feel that you can't focus. Just calmly bring your mind back to your meditation until your session is over. If you don't meditate for a day because you're too busy or not feeling well, forgive yourself. If you forget or become inconsistent with your practice, forgive yourself. Let go of the mistakes you make and move on.

Slowing down will also help you when it comes to meditation and mindfulness. You live in a fast-paced world, and this can make you feel like you need to get everything done as quickly as possible. Your day might start off in a rush because you need to get yourself ready for work and your children prepared for school. You might feel like you're running through your day until the moment you lay down to go to sleep. But then you start to find yourself tossing and turning because you can't turn off your thoughts.

Meditation is one of the best ways to start understanding and controlling your thoughts. When you find yourself focusing on a negative thought, you can direct it to leave your mind by thinking about something positive or that makes you happy. For example, visualizing your favorite vacation spot can help you turn your thoughts around because you will start to feel happy and relaxed, just as you felt on your trip. Think about your mind as a switchboard. Every time you make a connection, your thoughts will have a specific direction to go.

# 5

# THE POWER OF GRATITUDE

*"Gratitude is the healthiest of all human emotions. The more you express gratitude for what you have, the more likely you will have even more to express gratitude for."*

— ZIG ZIGLAR (SWEATT, 2016)

O ne of my friends called me in the middle of the night. As soon as I answered the phone, I knew something was wrong because I heard her crying on the other end. She was crying so hard for the first couple of minutes that she couldn't talk. It took everything in my power to not jump in my car and drive the two hours to her house, but I knew this wasn't the right answer. She didn't need me to panic. She needed me for another reason. So, I told her, "Go ahead and cry. I'm here, and I'll still be here when you're ready to talk."

After she calmed down enough to talk, she started explaining her increasing negative thoughts and the hold they had on her. She told me that her husband of several years threatened to leave her because she wasn't happy, and this didn't make him happy in their relationship. She told me that she still loved her husband, but she didn't know how to tell him. She couldn't think of ways to bring happiness back into their marriage. Feeling that her marriage was heading for divorce, she was willing to try anything and asked what advice I had.

I had several pieces of advice, and one was to write in a gratitude journal. She had never heard of this before, so I told her that it's taking time out of her day, just a few minutes, to write down what she is grateful for about that day. She could have a section in the journal that focuses on her marriage. She should write what her husband did that day to make her feel grateful for him and their relationship. I also advised that she try to get her husband to do the same thing. If he wasn't willing to write about it, she could just talk to him about it. She could start by reading her journal entry, and then he could respond by telling her what he is grateful for, with her and their relationship. From there, they need to keep their lines of communication open and focus on other bumps in their relationship.

She hung up the phone, telling me she would do her best. After a couple of weeks, I got another call from her. She said that the gratitude journal helped her mindset, and she was already starting to notice her thinking is changing throughout the day. She and her husband take time every night to talk to each other. Not only do they say what they're grateful for, but they also discuss any problems and are working on compromising.

It's been a couple of years since that first phone call, and they continue this pattern. Now, their nightly talks are their favorite part of their day, and their marriage is stronger than ever.

The main reason I told her about a gratitude journal is that it's one of the main steps I took that helped me create a positive habit with my thinking. Since I started my journal around four years ago, it's evolved to include the negative thoughts I had during the day and why I'm grateful for them. For example, I thought I was lazy one day because I laid around on the couch all day binge-watching Netflix. I kept telling myself to get up and do something useful, but I continued to lounge around.

As I wrote in my journal, I realized that I was grateful for my lazy day, and this thought, because it made me aware of how exhausted I felt from working so much during the week. If I'm not focusing on my career, I'm focusing on my family, home, and friends. I don't take the alone time that humans need, so this day my body forced me to take some time off. Of course, I still did a few household chores, but I didn't let them rule my day like I usually do when I don't have to work outside the home.

But this is only part of what gratitude can do for you. Even though the power of gratitude seems like a newer path toward healthier thinking, it's an old strategy that people have used for centuries. It's only gained more acceptance in recent years as studies continue to focus on how it helps people change not only their thinking but their way of life.

## HOW GRATITUDE WORKS

Like most people, you had a dream as a child. You may have imagined a comfortable, maybe rich, lavish lifestyle, a happy family, home, and a great social life. You take time to reflect on where you thought you'd be and where you are now and some-times wonder what happened. You ask yourself why you can't afford to buy your dream home or what you did wrong in your marriage.

Perhaps, you blame yourself for mistakes that you had little or no control over and lay in bed at night worrying about the future. Sometimes you wish for a break but feel that it will never come. Like many people, this is how you think all too often. It's why you focus heavily on reading morning affirmations or ignoring negative thoughts. This is one reason why you struggle with your thoughts on a daily basis. You know that you should think positively, but the negative thoughts keep coming. It's a familiar story for many people and one that gratitude knows all too well, which is why it works against it.

THE POWER OF GRATITUDE  |  85

Emotionally, gratitude is a powerful positive emotion that helps you feel at peace. It increases your overall health and gives you the motivation to work toward your highest self. It's a state of thankfulness. For example, it's the feeling you have when watching your children playing, enjoying a book, purchasing a new car, listening to music, and spending quality time with your partner, knowing that you have a home to go to after work, and have financial stability. It helps change your thoughts from negative to positive.

Positive psychology explains that gratitude works by acknowledging the good that happens in your life. Whether it's large or small, you're grateful for what you have. You also take time to find a reason to be thankful when times are tough.

Scientifically, gratitude works by changing certain parts of your brain. Studies prove that when you're grateful or happy, the right anterior temporal cortex is in the spotlight, which changes your brain activity. It also helps you look at situations in a more positive light because it helps decrease stress, anxiety, and depression. It is important to note that you may be naturally more grateful than someone else, giving you an advantage when learning gratitude techniques. Some people struggle to feel thankful, so it may take more time to develop gratitude as a daily living habit.

When you incorporate thankfulness into your life, toxic emotions are released from the chemicals in your brain. The part of the brain responsible for emotions is the limbic system, which consists of the hypothalamus, amygdala, thalamus, cingulate gyrus, and hippocampus. Collectively, these areas not only focus on emotions but also on memory and bodily functions (Chowdhury, 2019).

University of Southern California (Los Angeles) researchers, from the Brain and Creativity Institute, analyzed the brain's influence on gratefulness, morals, and values. They measured brain activity through functional magnetic resonance imaging (fMRI), focusing on moral cognition and value judgment. The participants were hooked up to the technology and then heard stories about holocaust survivors. They learned about the people who helped the survivors and how. The researchers then asked the participants to imagine how they would feel in a similar situation. They were to think about how they would react and feel. Afterward, researchers asked them to rate their level of gratitude.

The study concluded that the medial prefrontal cortex and anterior cingulate cortex showed heavy signs of brain waves, which are the areas that focus on value judgment and moral cognition (Ziogas, 2019). The key to this study is that it shows the more you focus on connecting yourself to others, the more gratitude you feel. For example, you might be grateful for your parents, who worked hard to provide you with a home during your childhood and helped send you through college. However, it's important to note that you don't need to think about someone else and their situation to feel grateful. You can bring yourself to a situation in your own life and respond in the same way.

Researchers from the University of California, Berkeley, conducted a study in 2003, focusing on the effects of gratitude writing. They looked at how expressing gratitude changes a person's physical and psychological health and attitude. They concluded that writing activities, such as journaling and writing letters of gratitude, improved mental well-being.

The research divided participants into three groups. The first group didn't have any writing activities during the course of the study. The second group received the instruction to write one letter of gratitude for three weeks. The third group wrote in a gratitude journal, examining their struggles, and writing about any negative thoughts and feelings they had during this time.

Ultimately, the second group felt more motivation to succeed and that they could more easily overcome obstacles. They reported better health for several weeks after the course of the study, as well. This study demonstrates that gratitude writing, whether in a journal or through another means, can help improve your mental and emotional health (Wong & Brown, 2017).

Even if you're not a writer or you've never tried to keep a journal, you might want to give gratitude writing a try. You don't need to focus on writing every day, but you can choose to sit down and reflect on your day three to four times out of the week. You might do this in the evening before you go to bed, as a way to focus on the positive aspects of your life. You can even choose to write a letter of gratitude to your friends and family members for some time. Once you write the letter, get in contact with the person, and ask them if they would like to meet to read the letter to them. Of course, it's also possible to send it through email, or the regular mail, especially if this makes you more comfortable.

When you become thankful for what you have in life, your relationships will improve. For example, you'll become more patient with the people around you, from your family members to coworkers. Because you feel happier in your life, this emotion will expand into other areas of your life, including other people. You'll start to feel the need to change the way you treat people, improving relationships. You will focus on better ways to communicate with your partner. You might even help your friends or family heal from painful areas in their life. For example, you're talking with your partner, and you come to learn that they don't feel you compromise with them. They believe they should agree to your terms because you can be stubborn and have difficulty seeing their side.

At first, you're hurt, and you want them to give you space. But, after a bit of reflection, you start to understand their side. Gratitude helps you open your eyes and mind so you can understand people better. Therefore, you can sit down with your partner and discuss better ways to communicate and handle disagreements beneficial to both sides. You feel more positive, so you know that it's essential to remain calm during an argument, even if it means you need to take a few minutes to yourself. You want other people to feel the same, so you'll do what you can to help them in this area. However, you understand you need to keep your mental health strong to retain the benefits of gratitude.

This helps you keep sight of your psychological well-being, making you less likely to feel stressed and overwhelmed. Several studies support the theory that gratitude strengthens your relationships. Some have shown that you're more likely to forgive other people, including yourself. Other studies found that you're less likely to argue with your partner and promote conflict resolution. Researchers also conclude that you have a stronger belief in connecting with other people and doing your best to reach a balanced level of satisfaction (Craig, 2019).

Researchers from Boston, for example, focused on how gratitude improves your physical health. In 2017, over 160 participants were measured for levels of depression, anxiety, optimism, thankfulness, and signs of heart disease. People who showed higher signs of optimism and gratefulness had fewer symptoms of heart disease. They also suffered less from depression and anxiety.

On the other hand, participants who didn't practice gratitude and also had higher levels of psychological illness showed more physical signs of heart disease (Ziogas, 2019). Science helps you understand the connection between the actions you take and the benefits you'll feel. Your health isn't just about what you put in your body; it also includes your behavior, emotions, and way of thinking. To help improve your overall well-being, you need to focus on what you're thankful for in your life, from your job to the people around you. Keeping an upbeat attitude will decrease your chances of cardiovascular disease, which can help you live longer.

## BENEFITS OF GRATITUDE

There are several benefits of gratitude. In fact, many people feel the list is endless because once they start thinking this way, they continue to come up with benefits. Some of them you'll feel as soon as you start focusing on your appreciative attitude. Other benefits will come into your life gradually. It's also important to note that everyone's chemistry is different, so you might not feel the same way as your friend, family member, or neighbor.

One of the most significant benefits is that gratitude enhances our mood. Practicing this thinking method helps you focus on your positive emotions, situations, and what you're grateful for. Naturally, this increases your happiness and makes you feel like you're fulfilling your life's mission. You'll become motivated to focus on your goals by taking them one step at a time and realizing that failure is okay.

Gratitude also enhances mood by decreasing depression and

anxiety. This happens because it starts shifting your thinking from negative to positive, making you feel better emotionally and psychologically. Instead of focusing on yourself internally, which can lead to negative thoughts, you start to look at external factors. You begin to appreciate what is in front of you, from physical objects and the environment to the people around you. For example, you're enjoying the sunshine as it beams through your window while drinking your hot cup of coffee.

Appreciation also increases your self-satisfaction, partly because it benefits your overall health. When you're satisfied, you're pleased with yourself. You are proud of what you've accomplished in your life, and you understand that some days will be harder than other days. This helps manage your thought patterns because you'll find yourself thinking that you can overcome obstacles, leading to a positive mindset.

When you can put things into perspective, by using gratitude, you're better able to evaluate your mental health and come up with a solution that is beneficial for you. For example, you might decide to take a personal day from work so you can unwind after trying to manage homeschooling, work, and a family. You'll focus on spending quiet time with yourself and peaceful quality time with your family. Once you realize that quality time alone is necessary for a healthy mindset, you'll find switching from negative to positive thoughts easily.

Gratitude can also act as stress relief; it can help control your anxiety. It's normal and healthy to have low levels of anxiety before certain events in your life, such as before speaking in front of a crowd or heading toward a job interview. The struggle you'll face comes when you allow worry to control your life, as then you might stop yourself from achieving your goals or completing a task. By regulating your stress, you can focus on your day-to-day routine without negative thoughts holding you back.

This doesn't mean you won't feel stressed or anxious at times. It just means that you can control this emotion easier because practicing gratitude can help you feel calmer and more relaxed. For example, you might go on a gratitude walk where you set a new goal to focus on the sounds, sights, and smells around you, or you can create a collage that focuses on what you're thankful in your life from your home to your well-being.

Another benefit is that your overall health improves. This means that you feel better psychologically, emotionally, and physically. It's important to note that all three of these factors work together when it comes to your functioning. For example, if you're sad or depressed, you won't take care of yourself in the same way when you're happy. People who aren't emotionally well won't eat healthy meals, they tend to exercise less, and they're more likely to think negatively. These actions weaken your immune system, which causes you to become sick.

But, when you think positively, you focus on eating healthy meals and exercise. You also take precautions to keep you from getting sick, and you focus on a self-care routine, which makes you feel emotionally and mentally stronger.

Gratitude can reduce pain but not just physical pain. It can reduce emotional and psychological pain as well. Sometimes you can become emotionally hurt and not feel anything physically. Other times you feel pain in several ways. No matter where your pain is, you can use meditation or other forms of gratitude to ease this feeling. You can learn to forgive the people who hurt you and find ways to move on from this pain. Gratitude allows you to heal because the positive emotions act like a warm blanket on a cold night. The key is to acknowledge the pain and how it developed so you can officially start moving forward.

You will look for people, events, and objects that inspire you. Sometimes this means that you listen to certain musicians who sing music that makes you feel good. Other times you might watch a movie or read a book that gives you a grateful feeling. You will start focusing on habits that make you feel good and give you a sense of peace. You can also feel inspired to do more with your life. For instance, you might write a book about your journey to help other people along their path.

Appreciating everyday moments in your life, and what you have, can help strengthen your skills. This ties into improving your overall health, concentration, and motivation. All of these factors help you notice how far you can go in life and allow you to thrive with your skills. For example, you're in a career where you have the option to continue your education. You think about how hard achieving your degree was for you, so you never thought about taking it a step further. Even though it would help you advance in your career, you always felt comfortable in your position.

Over the last few months, you've been meditating, counting your blessings, and practicing other forms of gratitude. This has increased your self-confidence, so you've been able to re-evaluate your college years. You realize that part of your problem in college was your partying. You didn't take college seriously until the last couple of years. You know that you would handle yourself differently now because you're motivated to improve yourself and your career. Therefore, you decide to take a leap of faith and find yourself thriving in college. You know you're well on your way to a promotion.

Finally, when you feel gratitude, you understand it's essential to do something that helps bring meaning into your life and the lives of others. You have an abundance of positivity that you want to share with the world and do what you can to make it a better place. You know that your community needs this more than ever, so you find volunteer work or a side job that you're passionate about. For example, you spend time supporting a local food pantry, get involved in the church, volunteer at a homeless shelter and support other nonprofits in your community. You might come to believe that this is your calling and change your career path, finding your new position more enjoyable, which only increases your happiness and reasons to be thankful.

## PRACTICE GRATITUDE

There are many exercises that you can perform throughout your day to help you practice gratitude. Some will only take a few seconds, while others might take a bit longer.

One of the first steps you should take is to start speaking kindly to yourself. The trick is you need to believe what you're saying. Sometimes your mind doesn't truly believe what you think. For example, you're working on a task at work and tell yourself, "I should be proud of what I've accomplished thus far." You look at the work you've completed, smile, and say, "I am proud of myself." But then your thoughts take you right back to how much work you have left to do. You then begin to feel anxious, wondering if you'll complete this project by the due date. This happens because you haven't made yourself genuinely believe that you're proud of the work you've done so far. Therefore, you need to take this a step further and tell yourself out loud. You need to stand in front of the mirror and say, "I am proud of the work I've completed thus far. I will finish the project on time because I'm a dedicated employee. I work hard, and I manage my time well."

Now, it's time to make this process a habit. Take time out of your day to stand in front of the mirror and say five good statements about yourself. They can be about your personality, how well you perform at work, or anything else. Each statement needs to be entirely positive. For example, "I am a good person. I have a lot of love in my heart. I am a great employee who is dedicated and works hard. I am a good parent. I am compassionate toward other people." You can decide to say something new every morning or the same five lines until you feel that you truly believe them.

You can also practice by starting a gratitude jar. All you need to do is find a jar, but a box will also work, and any supplies to decorate your container. For example, you can write your favorite quotes down, decorate it with pictures that make you happy, pour glitter all over it, or keep it simple and tie a ribbon to it. You will also need paper and a writing utensil. Then, you need to ensure you take time every day to drop a word, saying, or event into the gratitude jar. You can write something that you're grateful for that happened during the day or what someone said to you. Write as much or as little as you want. Over time, you'll find that the jar quickly fills up, and you can visually see all the reasons you have to feel thankful. A bonus is that you can read some of them when you need a little pick-me-up after a bad day, or you can't seem to find your appreciation of life. No matter how positive you feel, you'll always have negative days. The trick is finding a solution to bring yourself out of them.

Gratitude visits are a great way to show someone that you're thinking about them. Usually, this is done through a letter and dropping it off to the person physically. However, this isn't always possible because sometimes the person who makes you feel grateful is hours, states, or even countries away. In this case, you can email them, message them through social media, or write them a letter and mail it to them.

The first step of this practice is to think about someone that makes you feel grateful. This doesn't have to be a family member or friend. It could be a teacher, coworker, or someone you briefly met and made a difference in your life. Write or type the letter down. Don't think about what you're going to write, just think about the person and what they did for you. Take your mind back to the situation and remember how it made you feel. Explain to them how this moment helped influence your life and how you're still thankful for it. Put in as much detail as you care to share. You don't need to worry about punctuation or grammar. You need to worry about your emotion.

If you can physically visit the person, call them, and let them know you want to stop by. Set up a time and then be prompt. Put any embarrassing or worrisome thoughts aside and then read the letter to them. Notice their reaction and pay attention to them, so you know that they feel what you're saying. You can also do this through video chat if you can't physically see them.

Finally, take time to reflect on how the visit made you feel. You'll quickly notice that you become grateful every time you think about it, and you feel even more positive.

Another practice is to find a gratitude buddy. This is a person that you talk to often and share information that makes you and them feel happy. You don't need to see your buddy to talk to them physically. You can speak over the phone, text, private messaging, or video chat. You might even communicate in a variety of ways, depending on how you're feeling and how much information you want to share with them. You can talk to them about setting up a time or contact them randomly throughout the week, especially when your mind needs a little extra care. Of course, they can also contact you whenever they need to change their mindset.

The biggest key with this practice is you need to ensure the other person gets as much time as you do. It's easy to talk about all the good situations happening in your life when you're feeling positive. But this can cause issues when you don't let your partner talk, or they're not feeling as happy and don't care to communicate as much. Always notice how they're feeling and try to help them through any struggles. Like any relationship, one with a gratitude buddy is a two-way street.

The next time an unpleasant event happens to you, think about five good things that happened because of it. For example, you failed your college exam. You rarely get bad grades, so you feel that this class will be the hardest one of your college years. Even though it was the first exam, it was 20% of your grade, and you're worried about what it will do to your final grade. You continue thinking about this situation, and it drags you down to the point that you're having trouble focusing and studying for your other exams. It's at this moment you realize that you can learn from your bad grade, so you reflect on the reason you failed.

First, you realize that you didn't study like you usually do. Your friends went out to eat for dinner, and you wanted to tag along. You thought they'd go back to the dorms right away, but instead, they took you to the movies and then a walk around the city. You then realize that you got back to your room late, which is another contribution to your grade. Therefore, you conclude that you need to put your studies above everything else.

You consider this growth in self-discipline a positive result. A second positive result is that you became aware of skills that you lacked, such as telling your friend "no" politely. This allows you to focus on saying "no" and understanding you don't need a reason. Third, you know how to study for your professor's next exams to get a better grade. Fourth, you started keeping a planner so you can manage your study time better. Finally, you found a study buddy in the class. Through this one negative situation, you developed better study skills and became more confident as a student.

Another way to practice gratitude is to simply try to be grateful. You don't have to put much effort into it. All you need to do is think of things that make you happy. For example, your career, pets, family, friends, the smell of certain candles, music, and anything else. By putting a smile on your face with these thoughts, you'll increase serotonin production in your anterior cingulate cortex. You can also add them to your gratitude jar or write them down so you can quickly turn back to them in the moments you're struggling.

If you're a little more creative, you can focus on making a gratitude flower or collage. When you make a gratitude flower, you write down what you're grateful for on each petal. You'll need a pair of scissors, colored paper, marker, and tape or glue. You can use yellow to create the center of the flower, making it big as you want to. For the middle piece, write down, "What I am thankful for." You can use a template online to cut out the petals or make them any size and shape that you choose. You can even make heart-shaped ones; remember, this is strictly for you and your thought process.

When you're focusing on what to write on the flowers, think about situations, people, or objects in your life that make you feel happy. You can start by making a list and putting the items in a "high," "medium," and "low" category, so you know which ones to place on your petal first. You can add as many parts of the flower as you want, but you want to make sure that you can read every word on the flower. If you find that you don't have enough room, you can make another flower or switch to a gratitude tree. You can also make a collage. All you need is a poster board, pictures of what makes you grateful, glue, scissors to cut the images or phrases, and a place to hang it.

You always want to place any creative item in a spot where you will see it often. However, you can easily become used to seeing it, so it's vital to change location or take time to reflect on your flower/tree/collage when you're feeling down.

## JOURNALING

I have mentioned journaling throughout this book. Journaling can be a powerful tool for you in all aspects of mindfulness.

Using journaling is a great way to help you practice gratitude. One way to do this is by writing in your gratitude journal about certain "negative" events or moments in time, how they made you feel, what happened, and how you can appreciate these moments. You can write as much or as little as you want. The important thing is that you take this time to accept the negative events and focus on helping you grow mentally and emotionally.

Your self-satisfaction strengthens because you start focusing on how you can improve your life. A study conducted by Robert Emmons and Anjali Mishra in 2011 demonstrated that motivation increases with gratitude. Their research focused on college students who were asked to evaluate their goals over two months. They were told to write down what they wanted to accomplish; they were then placed into three groups for the next ten weeks.

The first group was told to complete one journal writing activity every week. The second group was told to count their blessings. The third group was instructed to list their challenges. The study concluded that the second group showed more determination to complete their goals than the other two groups (Armenta & Lyubomirsky, 2017). When you take the time to write in a journal, you'll not only feel more grateful, but you'll stay focused on your vision.

You will find that when your mind is at peace, you sleep better. You not only fall asleep faster, but you stay asleep as well. One of the main reasons you might have trouble falling asleep is because you're busy thinking about all the tasks you didn't complete, how you "should have" handled a disagreement, or all the mistakes you made. You might even find yourself going years back, thinking about how to mean you were to certain classmates in school.

When you take away these thoughts, your mind remains clear at night by focusing on gratitude practices, allowing you to drift into a deep sleep.

Many people think that you need to write in the journal every day for it to be effective. A study by psychologist Sonja Lyubomirsky and colleagues analyzed two groups of people. One group wrote in their gratitude journals three times a week for six weeks, while the second group completed this activity one day every week. Researchers concluded that participants who wrote once a week felt more grateful for their lives (Marsh, 2011).

It's also important to point out that you should never force yourself to write in your journal. The point of this exercise is to give you a task during the week to help boost your overall health, not to make you feel like you have a job to do. You can keep your supplies handy and write in them as you wish, even if you skip a week. You might also find yourself writing twice in one week and then not the next week.

One way to keep yourself in the habit of writing is to make it personal but focus on the positive. For example, write about the people that you're grateful for because of how they've impacted your life. Get as specific as possible, such as writing down the event and how it made you feel. For example, maybe you're grateful for a friend because they introduce you to new people and inspire you to eat healthily and exercise.

Suppose you're ever struggling with what to write in your journal, set up a system where you write about a particular category every day. For instance, one day, you'll write about relationships, and the next day you'll discuss an object near you. You might write about an opportunity you were given during the week on a different day and then choose to write on something you saw that made you happy or excited. You can always ask yourself questions to help you dig deeper, such as "What is the oldest relationship I am grateful or?" or "What is one characteristic of my partner that I'm grateful for?"

Make sure that you practice gratitude often. You should take time out of your day to ensure you are thinking happy and healthy thoughts. You want to do it in a way that's beneficial for you. Maybe writing in a journal every evening or sending a letter to a friend once a week.

There are many other ways that you can practice gratitude. For example, you can stop gossiping or speaking badly about people, even if you don't care for them. Instead, focus on those who inspire you and who love you unconditionally. Pick a day out of the week where you will not complain about anything. You can also start increasing the number of days you follow this process. Take time to think about other people who serve your community and thank them. For example, bring donuts to the police and fire department. Take time out of your day to compliment someone, whether it's a friend, family member, coworker, or someone in the store. If you notice someone who is having a tough day, give them a smile. Finally, take news and social media breaks or "vacations" to avoid negativity in the media.

## TIPS FOR STRENGTHENING THE POWER OF GRATITUDE

Now that you understand how gratitude works, its benefits, and how you can practice gratitude in your life, it's time to focus on strengthening your power. This is an essential step to incorporate into your life so you can continue to build positivity into your environment, mind, and body.

**When you're faced with challenges, find gratitude.** It's

important to realize that gratitude isn't only for positive experiences. In fact, you want to see it in the most challenging situations because it helps you focus on what is important and that you still have reason to be thankful. You can practice this tip by digging into your past to learn how specific life experiences helped you grow and become the person you are today.

**Don't be picky; appreciate everything.** This tip kind of ties into the first one. You don't just focus on the bigger situations in life; you want to appreciate everything, big and small. For example, this morning, I felt grateful that I started my mornings by tending to my tiny flower garden. It's good practice to look at what seems to be a meaningless situation and find a reason to appreciate it. Maybe you can give thanks for the sun shining or the chance to open your windows on a beautiful, clear day.

**Take time to volunteer.** Volunteering is a great way to give back to your community, help other people, and feel good about yourself. While most people want to give back during the holidays, it's important to find time to do this throughout the year. You can set up times to volunteer with various organizations around your community or visit the elderly in nursing homes. Listen to them as they tell you stories about their lives and give them a reason to smile.

**Express yourself.** Don't be ashamed to express how you feel and how grateful you are for the events in your life and the people around you. Sometimes you become so grateful that you can't keep it bottled up inside, nor should you! Your positivity can slide into someone else's heart and make them happy and grateful as well. Plus, when you express the way someone makes you feel, they feel good about themselves. An essential step of changing your thoughts is helping other people to think positively too.

**Practice mindfulness.** Continue to practice mindfulness exercises and meditation to help your mind feel more at peace and calm. The more you set this into your daily routine, the more gratitude you'll notice.

**Improve happiness in all areas of your life.** You might feel that some areas of your life are filled with negative emotions. Even if you can't find a reason to be happy in all aspects of your life, try to focus on one at the time and then continue this process. For example, you still struggle with emotions from your previous job because of how they treated you. This negativity has followed you into your current job, and now you're wondering how long you can mentally and emotionally handle working there. You start to feel stuck because you can't leave your position without finding a new career path. This is an area you can begin to improve, so you feel happier at work. You can complete this task by focusing on the people or tasks that you enjoy, or the fact that you have a job that helps you create a happy life.

**Take time to be with your loved ones.** If you find yourself struggling, spend time with your family and friends. They care about you and will try to do what they can to help you understand your feelings and make you feel better emotionally and mentally. Plus, sometimes you just need to sit back, relax, and have a little silly fun with someone you love. You can also take this time to practice gratitude with each other, similar to a gratitude buddy.

# 6

# THE POWER OF THE BODY

---

*"Go inside and listen to your body, because your body will never lie to you. Your mind will play tricks, but the way you feel in your heart, in your guts, tells the truth."*

— MIGUEL RUIZ (INFORMATIVE
QUOTES, 2015)

---

Y ou have probably heard the term "psychosomatic," which describes the interaction between your body and mind. Maybe you have learned that the mind affects the body, but did you know that the body can also have an effect on the mind? The mind and body; work together or against each other, just like any other partnership. Your body can speak to you to let you know how you truly feel, specifically regarding your emotional and mental well-being. For example, you get the "butterfly" feeling in your stomach when you're anxious or cry when you're feeling sad.

## WHAT THE RESEARCH SHOWS

For the last several decades, researchers have looked at the relationship between emotions and facial expressions. They want to understand how well people show how they feel and how outside factors can influence their expressions. One of the most prominent researchers in this area is Fritz Strack, from the late 1980s. For his study, Strack separated participants into two groups. The first group was asked to hold a pen between their lips while the second group held the pen between their teeth. Strack wanted to study how the emotions the groups felt would influence their facial expression.

The trick with the pen is that when held between your teeth, you look like you're smiling. When you hold it between your lips, you look like your frowning. He then gave the participants a comic book to read. Strack then asked them to rate the level of humor in the comic book. The study concluded by proving that the second group participants felt it was funnier than the first group. According to this study, your emotions can affect your facial expressions and vice versa. Even if the smile is "fake," you still feel happier and are more likely to find humor in the situation ("How Your Body Language Influences Your Thinking", n.d.).

In many ways, Strack opened the door for researchers to study body language and how it affects the mind. Over the last few decades, many experiments have looked at how posture impacts your state of mind. For example, when you're giving a presentation at work, you want to stand tall or with your back straight. You want to keep your hands visible without fidgeting and make eye contact with the audience.

What do you think about when you see someone slouching? Have you ever noticed what you think or feel when you sit in this position? While it's not a body posture that's focused on in many studies, researchers at San Francisco State University found that sitting in this position can decrease your mental health. It can make you feel sad or lack energy. Another conclusion of the study is that all you need to do to feel better is to sit in an upright position. Not only does this help your spine and can take away any pains, you start to feel, but it lifts your mood and increases concentration (Brinson, 2000).

Many new experiments have looked at power poses. These are body positions that show positivity, confidence, and self-assurance. These poses work because they increase testosterone by up to 20%; meanwhile, cortisol levels decrease, which indicates a de-stressing factor (Brinson, 2000). This pose involves keeping your hands on your hips, smiling, and sticking out your chest - standing tall and straight. You don't even have to do this in front of people. You can take a couple of minutes out of your day to power pose in front of a mirror to feel the benefits.

In the last study, we'll look at focusing on how walking impacts your state of mind. People walk in different ways, depending on their view of themselves and the environment around them. For example, if you're comfortable and confident, you're more likely to walk straight with your head held high. If you're uncomfortable, in a strange place, you're more likely to slouch when you walk and try to blend in with the crowd. You will lower your head and try not to make eye contact with other people.

This study took two groups of participants. The first group learned how to walk in an unhappy manner where they hung their shoulders and took heavy steps. The second group walked in a happy manner, where they took light steps with their back straight. The key is that neither group understood why they were walking in a certain way.

What the researchers found was that our posture not only influences our minds through emotions but also what we can remember ("How Your Body Language Influences Your Thinking," n.d.). According to the research, you can change your mood by altering your body language. For instance, when you apply yourself to a meaningful occupation, your body will begin to experience an emotion that you'll call "feeling good." This can involve any career that you're passionate about. Still, its levels are often heightened when you're in a manual labor type job because you're also getting regular exercise, which is necessary to help make your body feel better.

Many studies also show that you can use your body language to help your mind heal. You can use it to focus on feeling better emotionally and mentally. Simultaneously, it can also cause you more problems if you have poor or negatively viewed posture. For example, when you don't sit ergonomically correct, with your feet flat on the floor, you might lose focus easily or feel pain in your foot. The longer you sit in this position, the more negative your thoughts can become. But, once you sit up and start to take note of your posture, you'll become more motivated and feel more confident in your work.

Start to focus on power poses. Every morning for a couple of minutes, stand confidently in front of the mirror. You may not notice a big difference in your mood for the first few days, other than you might feel more motivated in the morning. But after about a week, you may start to notice your mindset changing. You might begin to see the tasks you need to accomplish and feel more confident knowing that you can complete them; you might have questioned your abilities in the past, but now you have more confidence.

## EXERCISING AND YOUR MIND

You know that exercise is good for your body and mind. Take a moment to think about a time when you exercised. It might

THE POWER OF THE BODY | 113

have been this morning or maybe a few months ago. Try to remember how you felt after completing the activity, even if it was just walking around your neighborhood. Do you remember what emotions you were feeling? Do you remember the sensations your body felt during the exercises? Even if you worked hard and felt tired after your session, your body and mind probably still felt energized. This feeling is useful when it comes to managing anxiety and even depression.

Exercise keeps you mindful. Even if you haven't used mindfulness techniques when you're in a session, you still pay attention to your body, so you don't overdo it or harm yourself. Next time you head to your gym or for a jog, take a moment to develop a mindfulness exercise strategy. For example, listen to your heartbeat and notice how it feels. What is the rhythm of your breathing? How does the wind or your clothes feel on your skin? By following this technique, you'll not only improve your physical condition, but you'll also interrupt any worries that pop into your head because it's so easy to "zone out" when you're exercising.

Exercise is excellent for depression. Through studies, researchers know that exercise acts almost like an antidepressant. Recently, the Harvard T.H. Chan School of Public Health asked participants to exercise for a period of time. Some participants were asked to run for at least 15 minutes, while others were asked to walk for about an hour. The study showed that both groups of participants decreased their risk of depression by up to 26% with regular exercise (Robinson et al., 2011).

If you struggle with depression, you'll find that some days are worse than others. For instance, you might feel depressed for a couple of months near the end of the winter season (usually referred to as seasonal depression) and then have a lot of energy and feel happy during the summer. You might also go through spurts of depression that last a few weeks and then find yourself relatively happy for a few months before another bout of depression comes. If this sounds like you, take time to exercise continuously. For instance, go out for a walk every morning or go to the gym three days a week. You don't have to spend a lot of time getting out and moving, but you want to ensure you spend at least an hour walking or 20 minutes of fast exercise.

Take a moment to think about the last time you felt stressed. Do you remember how your body felt? Were your neck and back muscles tight? Did you feel emotionally exhausted? Did you suffer from headaches or other aches and pains? There are many physical and emotional symptoms you can feel from stress. In fact, one reason why stress is so difficult to overcome is because of the way you feel physically, too. It's harder for you to fight stress when you're tired, feeling under the weather, or pain.

Other stress symptoms include trouble sleeping, heart problems, heartburn, frequent urination, diarrhea, and stomach aches. Stress creates a vicious cycle that will only cause you to feel more stressed, lose concentration, and contribute to depression, anxiety, and other problems that will hold you back from reaching your goals.

Thankfully, there is a way to break this cycle, and that's through exercise. This works because when you're continuously active for several minutes, your body releases endorphins in the brain. This helps relax your muscles, which relieves the tension in your body. Because your body and mind are a partnership, you start to feel better emotionally and mentally.

Research shows that when you start to move around once you feel negative emotions, your body starts to feel better, helping your mind feel more at ease. The trouble is you can find your mind wandering quickly, especially when you're exercising, which can lead you back to the negative thoughts. In this instance, bring yourself back into the present moment by focusing on your actions. For example, if you're lifting weights, what muscles are you using more than others. Focus on the part of the body that's getting the most benefit from your workout.

Then you start an exercise routine - start slow and simple. It's important not to put pressure on yourself when you're feeling down. Chances are, once you start, you will find your motivation to keep going. If you don't exercise often, or it's been a while, you'll want to begin gently, so you don't overdo it. Furthermore, it helps you when it comes to reaching your goal in a timely manner. For instance, if you don't usually go for a jog and decide you will run for an hour, you will become tired quickly. This will only add to your sadness and make you feel like a failure. But, if you decide to walk for an hour when you enjoy walking, and this is usually your form of exercise, you're more likely to succeed.

Second, you can simply get up and walk around your home for 15 to 20 minutes. You don't even have to go outside, though that's always one of the best steps to take as it can give you some sun and make you feel better. But, sometimes it's too cold, hot, or you're struggling physically. Get up and move about your home. Don't worry about stopping to complete any chores or talk to family members. You can even put on some music, walk up and down your steps, around your living room, and throughout your home. If you start to feel like you want to go outside to finish your exercise, go, and have fun. Sometimes you just need that little boost to get yourself going.

Third, do something that you enjoy. You don't need to get on the treadmill or run. You can always get on an exercise bike or even bike around your neighborhood. You can also drive out to the country and walk on a gravel road or find a nature trail. You might find that playing fetch with your dog is what gets you up and moving, which is the key. You need to find an activity that makes you want to get up and move. You might even want to tackle a home improvement project that is considered exercise, with heavy lifting or just moving constantly.

Finally, reward yourself. The trick is to not set the reward too high or the task too easy. For example, if you want to increase the amount of time you exercise, reward yourself when you add another five minutes to your routine and follow through with this amount of time for a week. You might decide to go out to the movies with friends or out to eat with your partner. Give yourself a reward that makes you want to reach your goal.

One of the most important tips when it comes to exercising is that you pay attention to your body. When you listen to your body and how you feel while exercising, you will know when you're pushing yourself a little too much. While it's good to increase your routine, you want to do this slowly. You don't want to cause your muscles to become overworked or harm yourself physically in any way, as this can damage your overall health.

## FINAL THOUGHTS ON USING YOUR BODY FOR POSITIVITY

Because body language and thoughts work together, you can use your body to improve your psychological well-being. Some of the ideas discussed here can make the difference between feeling positively or negatively about life. Let's quickly review:

### Smile!

One of the best ways to make yourself feel emotionally and mentally better is to smile more. There are many ways that smiling can make you feel better. For example, if you like your smile, you'll feel more attractive. This will give you an added boost of self-confidence, especially when you're presenting or talking to other people. Wearing a smile also means you are more likely to smile back from someone else, which always improves your mood. Finally, smiling helps you stay positive. Take a moment to smile and then think of something negative without losing your smile. It's difficult to think of something negative when you have a smile on your face. Now, think about how this smile made you feel. Did you feel happier?

## Straighten Up!

Another tip is to watch your body posture, so you don't start slouching. You know how this can affect your mindset, so it's best that you continue to sit up. You don't have to sit up straight because sitting in a relaxed position can help ease your mind. But you want to keep your spine and core as straight as possible. Not only will this help keep your posture strong, but it will also ease any painful pressure on your back. If you find yourself sinking into a chair while you're on your phone scrolling through social media or watching a movie, take a moment to sit up a little straighter and notice how your mood changes.

## Show Your Power

Maintain body positions that make you feel confident. Other than power poses and smiling, you can also walk straight, sit straight, and give a firm handshake. The more you focus on body language that shows other people you're a confident person, the more self-confidence you feel. From there, you'll start to improve your self-esteem and self-worth. This will only positively influence your life that will carry into your career, family life, and everywhere else. You'll start to focus on tasks that make you feel good and stop tasks that leave you feeling drained or with a lack of energy. You might also begin to eat healthier, and exercising could become more natural.

## Move

Keep yourself physically active. This goes beyond exercising. You want to get up and move at least every 30 to 45 minutes if you're sitting down. This not only helps improve your mood, but it can limit the amount of stress you put on your hips and lower back. Plus, it's not good for your heart to sit for an extended period of time. Sitting for an extended period is known to increase health problems. Keep your mind and body healthy by staying active. If you're at work, set a timer and get up every 40 minutes. Walk to the break room, use the bathroom, go say "hi" to a coworker, stretch, or walk outside and get a minute of sun time. You'll quickly feel your mindset change toward a positive direction when you're moving.

# HOW TO MAKE LASTING CHANGES
## IN THE WAY YOU THINK

*"Your attitude is critical to success. If you expect things to be difficult, it will always be easier to solve problems, overcome adversity, and have an enthusiastic energy about how you go about and enjoy your work."*

— NICK SABAN (DONNELLY, 2018)

To create a new, lasting thinking pattern, you need to remember it's normal to have thoughts of shame, doubt, fear, anxiety, and other negative emotions. The key is not to let yourself succumb to these thoughts. You need to find ways through practice, tips, and other means to rise above them. You might do this by meditating every morning, using a gratitude jar, talking to your buddy, or putting a smile on someone's face.

You want to do more than "do good things" to make you feel happy. You need to create habits that are sure to change your thinking pattern. They need to make an impression on your life, just like the people who are inspirational to you. Take a moment to think about your life's important events and how you continue to remember them and why.

You also need to have a "check in" time with yourself. It's important to reflect on where you are in life and how you feel emotionally, physically, and mentally. You can also focus on your spiritual health. This doesn't necessarily focus on your faith, but how well you're doing compared to your higher self, however, you define that. Everyone has the ideal person they want to become. For example, you want to be a straight-A student in school, become the manager of a company, or spend your time helping people through volunteering. Try to think of your higher self and reflect on what you can do to reach this person. The more you feel you're connected to your best self, the happier you become.

When you're checking in, make sure to look at your overall health in detail. How are you feeling emotionally and mentally? Is there something that is bothering you? Do you think that you're sinking into a depression? Notice any triggers that are affecting you and why. Learn how you can manage these instances and change the way you react to them. Remember, you can't change the way other people react, but you can always change how you see and react to things.

You might find that it's easier to find a quiet spot to reflect during this time. Go somewhere that makes you feel at peace; this will help you through any moments of negativity. If you come across bad thoughts, release them at that moment. For example, if you're in nature, close your eyes and allow your face to feel the sun's warmth. Imagine the negative thoughts dissolving in your body due to the heat on your face. You can also visualize the negativity leaving your body every time you exhale.

Don't force yourself to do anything that makes you feel overwhelmed or causes you to lose focus. Of course, there are times when you feel like you need to continue with a project. Taking a break (even if it's just a minute or two) can help clear your mind. It can also help you recharge your batteries so you feel that you can keep working on the task at hand.

Another trick is to make sure that you don't have too many distractions. This seems to become harder as the years go on, especially when you find yourself working online all the time and drifting toward your social media accounts, Google, YouTube, or Netflix. But you can't let distraction ruin your flow. Your brain is wired to follow a particular pattern; constantly losing focus can cause you to feel tired easily and lose interest in the project.

Maybe you need to establish working hours and set breaks. You might need to put your phone in the next room, which will keep you from looking at it too often. You can also put everything on silent, so notifications don't draw your attention away from what's important.

Never be afraid to reach out for help. You can contact your gratitude buddy or someone else to talk to. You can even seek professional advice if you need additional support. They can help you find the best way to get your thought patterns onto a better track without feeling like you're turning your life upside down. They can also go through gratitude practices with you and help you understand guided meditations and how to follow them. Don't be afraid if you feel you need help learning how to meditate, it's not the most natural process; your mind isn't wired to clear itself of certain thoughts.

When you start a new healthy habit, you want to create a ritual that will help you stick to the practice. For example, if you decide to incorporate meditation into your morning routine, you need to establish a different method. You decide that you will get up a half-hour earlier to prepare yourself for meditation and have time for the process. For a couple of weeks, you stop getting up earlier and soon find yourself pushing aside your meditation. You wonder what happened, so you analyze the situation. It's then you notice that you felt too tired to get up because you don't get enough sleep. Therefore, you decide the best course of action is to go to bed earlier to get up earlier. A month later and you find that you're not getting up a half-hour earlier but two hours earlier. You feel this is a positive change in your lifestyle because you don't feel as rushed in the morning, and you get quality time to yourself before your busy day. The benefits you feel from your new routine help you stick to your meditation.

It's important to note that just because you started a new routine doesn't mean you will continue to follow through with the habit every day or that you'll never return to your old way of thinking. Negative thoughts are common. Your brain is wired to think negatively over positively, as we've mentioned, which is why changing your thoughts is harder than you might think. The key is that, when you have negative thoughts, you don't dwell on them. Instead, you accept them, and you move on. Take time to visualize removing them from your mind and releasing them into the air where they dissolve. You can do this by taking a deep breath or just pushing the thought out of your mind.

Along with self-acceptance, you need to practice self-compassion. This is naturally a bit harder when you realize you have negative thoughts. You start to ask yourself what happened and why you're thinking this way. While the reflection is good, as it can help you understand, you don't want to label yourself or talk down to yourself. Instead, you want to take time to say something like, "It's okay that I had this thought. It's part of what's going on in my life right now. There is no need to worry. I'll let this thought come as-is and then let it leave my mind. I'm stronger than this thought." You can also tell yourself, "Be kind, don't worry. Negative thoughts happen. In and out it goes."

## PROTECTING YOURSELF FROM NEGATIVITY

You know that you can control your behavior and thoughts, but you can't control anyone else. Even when you try to control your children, employees, or partner, you find that they do what they want, and you need to work with it. While it's easy to compromise with your family and friends, it's harder to work with people you don't know and bring constant negativity into your environment.

The truth about negativity is that it's draining. It drains the positivity out of your body because it needs to make room for itself. Think of it this way—you can only have so much energy in your body. So, when you're full of positivity, the negativity needs to kick some of that out to make room for itself. Then, it starts inviting other negative feelings and thoughts into your body, kicking even more positivity out. This is why when you focus on bringing positive energy in; you remove the negative first. You need to create room for good feelings as well. You can use this thought to your advantage when it comes to protecting yourself from the bad emotions and environment surrounding you.

One of the first steps you can take is to set limits. Set limits with negative people because they will always find someone to wallow their problems too. Misery loves company, after all. It's hard for anyone always to feel stressed and have troubling thoughts, so they need someone that they can vent to. While listening to them, especially if they're friends and family, have your own mental health in mind. When they're talking to you, their negativity automatically enters your body and fills your mind. In return, you can start thinking dark thoughts. Practicing mindfulness can be beneficial here. While you're helping them to vent, you can visualize their negativity bouncing off of you. Even though you're listening to them, you can also focus on your own self, making sure that you're not absorbing their negativity.

If it starts to feel overwhelming, you can also introduce a pleasant topic to the conversation - simply change the subject. For example, your friend talks about their angry coworker and how challenging they are to work with. You listen to them for a few minutes and then realize they're becoming more frustrated as time goes on. You also notice that they keep repeating their thoughts, and you're starting to feel the same way. In fact, you notice that you're increasingly becoming annoyed by their words. Because you don't want to react irrationally, you decide to change the topic entirely. The key is finding a way to introduce the topic without making them feel like you're trying to ignore their feelings.

One way to do this is by telling them that you understand the way they feel, and you hope the situation gets better. You can then explain ways they can improve their situation, including setting their own boundaries. From there, you can bring in a lighter topic by showing them the benefits the steps they take can have on their emotional and mental health. After this, it becomes easier to bring up any light and fun topic to help make them smile and laugh, so they have a better day. Another way is by telling them a funny story that relates to the topic. Once they start feeling better, they'll quickly change their thoughts and come up with other lighter topics.

You always need to remember that you can't control someone else; you can't control the way they think or feel. Instead, you can try to help them focus on a more peaceful mindset. You can only give them time and your ear - after that, it's up to them. They need to take action. It's not always easy to take a step back and realize this, especially when it's your family or a close friend who is struggling. However, you need to let go of the desire to change someone else's mindset. You need to do your best to accept where they are in their life and support them the best you can. You can't save them – however, you can show them support as they take the steps they need.

There are other people in your life that I refer to as energy vampires. They will try to do everything in their power, usually through manipulative tactics, to drain of your positive energy. I refer to them as energy vampires because you can feel them sucking your energy as they talk to you. For example, you will start to feel emotionally drained and physically tired. They will often try to manipulate or blackmail you into doing what they want, which is staying around them, so they can continue to take your energy. They want you to feel as badly as they feel -

and, although this is rarely a conscious action on their part, that's what helps them feel "better."

Protect yourself by focusing on solutions instead of problems. People who think negatively will come to you with multiple problems but no solutions. When you try to talk to them about what to do, they will brush you off or tell you that it won't work. At this point, you need to take one of two steps. First, you can remove yourself from the situation. This is the best course of action to take when you start to feel frustrated or angry. Your second choice is to continue to work with them on a solution until they begin to feel confident that one will work. This is not an easy step but also not impossible. The key is not to let yourself become overwhelmed. You need to remain calm and try to understand their frustration.

Another challenge that comes with negative people is their impression of you. They rarely shy away from telling you what they think because it gives them an outlet to get rid of their challenging emotions and thoughts. The trick is to maintain a level of emotional detachment with them, so you don't become too involved with their opinion of you. This doesn't mean that you won't feel a tinge of hurt, guilt, frustration, or sadness. It doesn't mean that the words won't initially affect you. But it does mean that you can quickly move the words out of your mind because they don't necessarily matter. Don't take them to heart.

If you take what they say to heart, you are giving them control of your emotions, and ultimately your ability to be happy. It's at this moment you start leading yourself down a path of negativity and need to reroute your thoughts to focus on the positive again. The biggest challenge you face when it comes to someone's opinion of you is how close you are to the individual. For example, if it's an acquaintance or coworker who says something, you probably won't take it as personally as when a friend or a family member says something hurtful.

Realistically, however, it's people who are closest to you that usually criticize you in a harsh manner. Other people tend to choose their words carefully or watch what they say because they aren't as close to you. People who are close feel more comfortable saying something that could hurt you and decrease your self-confidence, even for a moment. Therefore, you need to make sure that you're in control of your thoughts and emotions, no matter who is talking to you.

You also need to be aware of signs that negative people are starting to take control of your mind. One way to do this is to notice when you start going back to your old habits. For example, if you lay awake at night thinking about your mistakes and worrying about the future and find yourself starting this again, it's time to take a step back from people who are bringing negativity into your life.

A dear friend of mine had to "walk away" from one of her aunts. Her father's sister had always been difficult, but my friend has a deep sense of family obligation, so she wanted to show love and care for her elderly aunt. A few years ago, her aunt asked her to come to help her with some household improvements. My friend drove for two days, by herself, to help out her aunt. During the two weeks that she was there, painting the house, trimming back trees and bushes, and helping with some neglected repairs, her aunt was verbally and emotionally abusive. She tried to tell her aunt to be gentler, but things kept getting worse.

Finally, after her aunt screamed at her because she wasn't raking the leaves "the right way," my friend had had enough. She calmly put the rake down, cleaned up the tools she had been using in the backyard, and informed her aunt that she would be leaving in the morning. "I didn't drive all this way to be yelled at. I came here to help you because I love you." Her aunt gave her the silent treatment after telling her she was "acting like a child." My friend took a deep breath, packed her things, tried to hug her aunt goodbye (but was shunned), and left that afternoon.

"It was hard," my friend shared with me. "I wanted to help my aunt because I know that she had been through a lot these last few years - losing her husband and having a tough time keeping the house in repair. But I couldn't take it anymore - I still love her, but I have put some emotional distance between her and me. This means that we're not in contact much. Instead, I chose to focus my love and attention on members of my family and friends, who appreciate me and love me as much as I love them."

When dealing with people like my friend's aunt, it's essential to take a few steps back and ask yourself some questions. For example, "Am I hurt?" "Am I really a bad person?" "I can't believe they talked to me like that, did I deserve it?" or "Am I doing the right thing?" When you start to notice you're questioning yourself in this manner, it's time to put your boundaries back up and take a few steps back from the person who is making you feel this way. If being around someone makes you ask these types of questions, they are not suitable for you. There are plenty of people who would never make you feel that way. Focus on them, and surround yourself with people who treat you well.

## STEPS TO CREATE CHANGE IN YOUR LIFE

It's time to focus on creating a plan of steps that you will follow to keep the positive change in your life going strong. Here is an example plan that you can follow:

1.  You want to assess where your life is sitting now and how you're mentally, physically, and emotionally done. Look in the mirror and ask yourself, "What do I see in myself?" Do you see a compassionate person working hard and staying motivated to move up in their career? Do you see someone who is struggling with their

thoughts and might need additional help to overcome negative thinking? Be honest with yourself when you answer how you're doing and how well you handle certain negative situations. Analyze the good and bad answers you give. Don't worry if you notice you're thinking more negatively than you thought. It's a long process when you start changing your mindset. It's also a process that you will work on for the rest of your life. While it will become easier, it's always a focus in your daily life.

2. Accept yourself for who you are. Remember, everyone has negative thoughts at times, no matter how positive or optimistic they seem. You are who you are, and you need to be proud of this person to move on to greener pastures. You are working toward reaching your goals and becoming a better person. This takes time, so you always need to be proud of who you are.

3. Always take responsibility for your actions. Everyone does something that they regret later, so you shouldn't dwell on these moments. Instead, take responsibility for what you are doing or not doing and how this affects you and other people. Learn from your mistakes and move on.

4. You will always have something in your life that you want to change. The key is to focus on changing the things that you have control over. Look at where you are now and think about what you want to change. Do

you want to increase your self-compassion? Do you want to go back to school? Write down what you want to change, and any ideas you have that can send you on a path in this more positive direction.

5. But you need to do more than write down ideas. You need to commit to that change. Put your ideas into actionable steps that you can accomplish. You need to make the decision that you will change and follow your goal to accomplish this change. No one can make you follow this path but yourself, so it's essential to find a way to act.

6. If you need to seek help to set yourself down a path of success, do so. You can contact friends, family members, or therapists to help you. Educating yourself is one of the most important steps toward success, so read and study self-help manuals, like this one, to help you come up with ideas to change your life and your thinking.

7. Make sure you keep self-compassion in mind. You will have days when you don't reach your goals, and you will have weeks when you fall back into negative thinking. Accept that it happened and tell yourself that it's okay. Be gentle with yourself and focus on how you can continue committing to a more positive lifestyle.

8. Always take time to reflect. You don't need to do this every day, but you should do it several times a week. Think about the progress you've made and where

you're heading. Go over your goals again and make sure you understand all the action steps you've set for yourself to achieve. You can even take this time to give yourself a little pep talk to keep yourself going.

9. Control the people around you. You can't control how people act when they're around you, but you can control who you spend your time with. If you want to bring more positivity into your life, you need to surround yourself with positive people who will also support your efforts. They will not only have a positive influence on your life, but they will support you during the difficult times, whether it's giving you advice, strength to move forward, or helping you step outside of your comfort zone. They will also focus on your best traits, helping you discover the best parts of yourself, which will improve your self-esteem.

# CONCLUSION

"*If you put negative thoughts into your mind, you're going to get negative results. It's just as true that if you put positive thoughts in your mind, you will be a recipient of positive results.*"

— LOU HOLTZ (DONNELLY, 2018)

The main purpose of this book was to help you understand that turning negative into positive thoughts is more than just flipping a switch. You need to follow certain powers that will strengthen your mind and soul. You understand the importance of mindfulness, gratitude, and your body. Now, it's time to put everything you've learned from this book into practice. The key is to realize that you're in complete control of your behaviors. No one can take action for your mindset; you need to take action yourself.

There are several key takeaways. First, it's vital that you remember you need to follow your path. You can choose any of the gratitude practices, meditations, and mindfulness exercises to help you along your journey. But you also need to be aware of how they make you feel. When you try a new practice, reflect on how you think and feel about the exercise. While you shouldn't disregard it after the first try, you might find that it's not the right one for you at this moment.

For instance, maybe you're focusing on meditating every morning and start with the guided meditation for healing. After trying to reach a meditative state for 10 minutes, you give up and think this practice isn't for you. The fact of the matter is you can meditate; you just need to focus on guided meditation for breathing first. You need to find a meditation ritual that will help you strengthen your breathing technique.

Another key is to remember it's okay to seek outside help, beyond your friends and family. Many therapists are willing to meet with you to help you understand your mental health during this time, including how it affects your overall health. They will guide you to solutions and help you focus on meditation, writing in a gratitude journal, or focusing on your body's power. They will help you understand your underlying reasons for any depression, anxiety, or other mental health issues. They will also help you set up a personalized plan to begin taking back control of your life.

The main reason people struggle with therapists is that they don't find the right one. Just because a therapist has high credentials and is excellent in their career doesn't mean that they're the best fit for you. It's essential that you find a counselor who has experience with your mission, one who makes you feel comfortable so you can break down your barriers and fully open up to them. After your first meeting, reflect on your time together. Even though it's only about an hour, ask yourself a series of questions to determine if you should continue the relationship or find a different therapist. If they are professional, they will always understand if you choose to go elsewhere.

You also need to take your time when it comes to choosing your thoughts. You need to go at your pace and understand that it might take you years to reach your desired outcome. You might try several practices and tips before you find a routine that works for you. Never rush or force yourself to think positively because this is when it backfires. Instead, you need to learn to acknowledge and accept your negative thoughts and analyze them. Why did these words come to you? Why do you feel this way? Were there triggers that caused them? Is it something that you should look further into or just move on from?

Remember, there is a very strong science behind your power to take control of your thoughts. By controlling your thoughts and turning them from negative to positive, your overall health -

including spiritual, emotional, and physical aspects of health - will improve. Focus on creating new pathways in your brain - from positive self-talk to change how you sit and stand - these simple changes can, quite literally, rewire how you respond to things. In the past, when you may have had immediate negative responses to something hurtful that someone says, now you can shrug it off, and understand that it's more about themselves than it's about you and your true self.

You've already come a long way in learning how to choose your thoughts. You've learned a variety of strategies and understand that they're entirely in your control. You're making powerful waves into your new positive lifestyle, and you need to be proud of yourself. For every step, you take, congratulate yourself. Above all, ensure that you put your mental health first. It's not always easy, but it's one of the most important pieces of you. Take care of yourself and your thoughts so you can take care of your loved ones, friends, and neighbors. By taking care of yourself, you can start to make the world around you a better place.

I appreciate your choosing my book to help improve your mindset and lifestyle. I am honored to be a part of your new positive path, and I send you all my best wishes. I hope this book gave you a guiding light for your path, and you continue to find it useful as you work toward your goals. Please take the time to review my book so you can help others learn how to choose their thoughts.

# REFERENCES

7 Negative Effects of Lack of Self-Confidence on Your Career |
Blog | Elite World Hotels. (n.d.). Www.Eliteworldhotels.-
Com.Tr. Retrieved May 27, 2020, from https://www.
eliteworldhotels.com.tr/blog-en/7-negative-effects-of-lack-of-
self-confidence-on-your-career.3509.aspx

10 Steps to Create Lasting Change in Your Life. (2013, January
31). Tiny Buddha. https://tinybuddha.com/blog/10-steps-to-
create-lasting-change-in-your-life/

21 Deep Quotes on Positive Thinking. (2016, May 20). Bright
Drops.        https://brightdrops.com/deep-quotes-on-positive-
thinking

Alton, L. (2017, November 15). Why low self-esteem may be
hurting you at work. NBC News; NBC News. https://www.

nbcnews.com/better/business/why-low-self-esteem-may-be-hurting-your-career-ncna814156

Armenta, C. N., & Lyubomirsky, S. (2017, May 23). How Gratitude Motivates Us to Become Better People. Greater Good. https://greatergood.berkeley.edu/article/item/how_gratitude_motivates_us_to_become_better_people

Aura: Meditation & mindfulness. (n.d.). App Store. Retrieved July 13, 2020, from https://apps.apple.com/au/app/aura-meditation-mindfulness/id1114223104

Baines, W. (n.d.). A Guide to Making Lasting Changes in Your Life. Www.Beliefnet.Com. Retrieved June 2, 2020, from https://www.beliefnet.com/inspiration/a-guide-to-making-lasting-changes-in-your-life.aspx

Brinson, S. (2000). 6 Ways Your Body Language Affects How You Think. Keepinspiring.Me. https://www.keepinspiring.me/6-ways-your-body-language-affects-how-you-think/

Bruce, J. (2013, November 13). How Positive Thinking Creates More Problems Than It Solves. Forbes. https://www.forbes.com/sites/janbruce/2013/11/19/how-positive-thinking-creates-more-problems-than-it-solves/#7ae17b98df73

Calm. (2014). Calm Blog. Calm Blog. https://www.calm.com/blog/about

Chernoff, A. (2015, September 3). 7 Ways to Protect Yourself from Other People's Negative Energy. Marc and Angel

Hack Life. https://www.marcandangel.com/2015/09/02/7-ways-to-protect-yourself-from-other-peoples-negative-energy/

Cho, J. (2016, July 14). 6 Scientifically Proven Benefits of Mindfulness and Meditation. Forbes. https://www.forbes.com/sites/jeenacho/2016/07/14/10-scientifically-proven-benefits-of-mindfulness-and-meditation/#41be459c63ce

Chowdhury, M. R. (2019, April 9). The Neuroscience of Gratitude and How It Affects Anxiety & Grief. PositivePsychology.Com. https://positivepsychology.com/neuroscience-of-gratitude/

Craig, H. (2019, March 3). The Research on Gratitude and Its Link with Love and Happiness. PositivePsychology.Com. https://positivepsychology.com/gratitude-research/

Donnelly, D. (2018, October 4). 20 Motivational Quotes on the Power of Positive Thinking. Sports for the Soul. https://www.sportsforthesoul.com/20-motivational-quotes-the-power-of-positive-thinking/

familydoctor.org editorial staff. (2018, February 15). Mind/Body Connection: How Emotions Affect Health. Familydoctor.Org. https://familydoctor.org/mindbody-connection-how-your-emotions-affect-your-health/

Firestone, L. (2013, June 13). The Power of Choosing Your Thoughts. Psychology Today. https://www.psychologytoday.

com/intl/blog/compassion-matters/201306/the-power-choosing-your-thoughts

Getting Started with Mindfulness - Mindful. (2018). Mindful. https://www.mindful.org/meditation/mindfulness-getting-started/

Guided Mediation Scripts. (n.d.). Retrieved May 27, 2020, from https://edswellness.org/wp-content/uploads/2017/01/Guided-Meditation-Scripts.pdf

Harbinger, J. (2019, February 18). The Downside to Our Upside: The Problem with Positive Thinking. Jordan Harbinger. https://www.jordanharbinger.com/the-negative-consequences-of-accentuating-the-positive/

Headspace Inc. (2012, February). Headspace: Meditation & sleep. App Store. https://apps.apple.com/us/app/headspace-meditation-sleep/id493145008

How to stop negative self-talk. (2017). Mayo Clinic. https://www.mayoclinic.org/healthy-lifestyle/stress-management/in-depth/positive-thinking/art-20043950

How your body language influences your thinking. (n.d.). NeuroNation. https://www.neuronation.com/science/how-your-body-language-influences-your-thinking

Informative Quotes. (2015, September 19). Go inside and listen to your body. Informative Quotes. http://www.informativequotes.com/go-inside-and-listen-to-your-body/

Insight Network, Inc. (2020). Insight timer. Insighttimer.Com. https://insighttimer.com/

Insight timer - meditation app. (n.d.). App Store. Retrieved July 13, 2020, from https://apps.apple.com/us/app/insight-timer-meditation-app/id337472899

Kaufman, C. Z. (2011). Here are six common career-limiting beliefs and how you can reframe them in a more constructive light. Monster Career Advice. https://www.monster.com/career-advice/article/career-limiting-beliefs

Keane, M. (2018, October 1). Mindfulness and your brain. A Lust For Life - Irish Mental Health Charity in Ireland. https://www.alustforlife.com/tools/mental-health/mindfulness-and-your-brain

Lawson, K. (n.d.). What Impacts Relationships? Taking Charge of Your Health & Wellbeing. Retrieved May 27, 2020, from https://www.takingcharge.csh.umn.edu/create-healthy-lifestyle/relationships/what-impacts-relationships

Maclean-Hoover, P. (2015, September 8). Good to Know: Why We Think the Way We Think. GoodTherapy.Org Therapy Blog. https://www.goodtherapy.org/blog/good-to-know-why-we-think-the-way-we-think-0908155

Marsh, J. (2011). Tips for Keeping a Gratitude Journal. Greater Good. https://greatergood.berkeley.edu/article/item/tips_for_keeping_a_gratitude_journal

Minden, J. (2016, August 25). The Problem with Positive Thinking. Psychology Today. https://www.psychologytoday.com/intl/blog/cbt-and-me/201608/the-problem-positive-thinking

Montell, A. (2019, August 9). A Psychologist Explains the Trouble with Positive Thinking. Byrdie. https://www.byrdie.com/positive-thinking-psychologists

Nazari, S. (2017, October 24). Are You Paralyzed by Overwhelming Feelings? Stop Procrastinating. GoodTherapy.Org Therapy Blog. https://www.goodtherapy.org/blog/are-you-paralyzed-by-overwhelming-feelings-stop-procrastinating-1024175

O'Connor, M. (2019, December 6). Meditation increases blood flow in the heart, PET scans show. Www.Healthimaging.Com. https://www.healthimaging.com/topics/cardiovascular-imaging/meditation-increases-blood-flow-heart-pet

Robinson, L., Segal, J., & Smith, M. (2011). The Mental Health Benefits of Exercise: The Exercise Prescription for Depression, Anxiety, and Stress. Helpguide.Org. https://www.helpguide.org/articles/healthy-living/the-mental-health-benefits-of-exercise.htm

Sarkis, S. A. (2011, September 9). 43 Quotes on Body Language. Psychology Today. https://www.psychologytoday.com/us/blog/here-there-and-everywhere/201109/43-quotes-body-language

Selva, J. (2019, July 4). 76 Most Powerful Mindfulness Quotes: Your Daily Dose of Inspiration. PositivePsychology.Com. https://positivepsychology.com/mindfulness-quotes/

Siegel, D. (2010, September 7). The Science of Mindfulness - Mindful. Mindful. https://www.mindful.org/the-science-of-mindfulness/

Smith, E.-M. (2019, June 19). What is Negative Thinking? How It Destroys Your Mental Health | HealthyPlace. Www.Healthyplace.Com. https://www.healthyplace.com/self-help/positivity/what-is-negative-thinking-how-it-destroys-your-mental-health

Suttie, J. (2018, October 29). Five science-backed reasons mindfulness meditation is good for your health. Mindful. https://www.mindful.org/five-ways-mindfulness-meditation-is-good-for-your-health/

Sweatt, L. (2016, November 24). 15 Thoughtful Quotes About Gratitude. SUCCESS. https://www.success.com/15-thoughtful-quotes-about-gratitude/

Walton, A. G. (2015, February 9). 7 Ways Meditation Can Actually Change the Brain. Forbes. https://www.forbes.com/sites/alicegwalton/2015/02/09/7-ways-meditation-can-actually-change-the-brain/#403e2b331465

Warren-James, N. (2019, November 5). How to prevent negative thoughts ruling your life. South China Morning Post. https://www.scmp.com/better-life/well-being/article/

3027600/negative-thoughts-can-impact-your-mood-mental-health-and

Wayne, R. (2018, July 13). Why Positivity Culture is A Problem. Medium. https://medium.com/@rachelwayne/why-positivity-culture-is-a-problem-f55aac748461

White, I. (2009, December 10). The mind affects the body, but can the body affect the mind? -. WellBeing Magazine. https://www.wellbeing.com.au/mind-spirit/mind/the-mind-affects-the-body-but-can-the-body-affect-the-mind.html

Wong, J., & Brown, J. (2017, June 6). How gratitude changes you and your brain. Greater Good. https://greatergood.berkeley.edu/article/item/how_gratitude_changes_you_and_your_brain

Ziogas, G. J. (2019, December 6). How Gratitude Rewires Your Brain and How to Make It Work for You. Medium. https://medium.com/change-your-mind/how-gratitude-rewires-your-brain-and-how-to-make-it-work-for-you-894e8bf73c59